Biography

Lucinda Williams

A Life in Lyrics and Melodies

Chapter 1

During the summer, my father would drink gin and tonic. When I was a kid, he would ask, "Honey, can you go make me a drink?" I knew how to pour gin into a shot glass and then into a cocktail glass filled with ice, followed by tonic and a piece of lime. Nobody back then thought that was a negative thing. I recall reading an article on Eudora Welty that described how she would drink one small glass of whiskey in the late afternoons before dinner. It was her small indulgence, a chance to unwind at the end of the day with a cocktail. In the same way, my father and my stepmother, Jordan, whom I affectionately referred to as Momma Jordan or Momma J, would drink a glass of wine or a cocktail at the end of the day, while my father opened the day's mail and we discussed current affairs or anything else. We would sit in the sunroom off the main room. It was completely glass, and it seemed like you were sitting outside. You could use that room all year because you didn't have to worry about bugs, but you could still enjoy the natural light. In the winter, it would be ideal because there was a potbelly heater outside to keep the room warm.

I had many experiences with my mother and her drinking. She wasn't a social drinker. She drank in private, as a closet drinker. I didn't notice this until I was about eighteen years old, when I was visiting my mother in her New Orleans apartment and she came to the door slurring her words. For years, she said it was due to her meds. I was used to seeing her that way. She had spent a lot of time in mental health facilities and treatment clinics, and she was taking drugs. However, during this stay with her in New Orleans, I immediately realised that she was also heavily drinking. I didn't realise she was an alcoholic until then.

Her mental disorder deprived her of her mother's instincts and abilities. We were close till she died in 2004, but after that, I stopped depending on her for anything. I realised at a young age that I would not receive from my mother what most children do: stability, warmth, dependability, and support. I never felt pressure from her, either. I mean, she lacked that capacity.

In retrospect, she is responsible for many of my positive characteristics. She read everything. She played the piano and listened to good music. She adored Judy Garland, Erroll Garner, and Ray Charles. She also introduced me to Joan Baez and Leonard Cohen. As I grew older and more conscious of her mental condition, I began to draw parallels between her position and that of Sylvia Plath, and in many respects, Anne Sexton. Plath and Sexton committed suicide. My mother did not commit suicide, but she did check out in other ways, at least from the perspective of her children.

My mother's name is Lucille Fern Day, and she was born on December 31, 1930. Her parents were Reverend Ernest Wyman and Alva Bernice Coon Day. She went by Lucy. Her father was a Methodist clergyman, so strict that you would believe he was a Baptist. He was a hellfire and brimstone evangelical preacher. Every two or three years, the Methodist Church relocated him to a different town in Louisiana. My grandfathers were both Methodist ministers, but my mother's family had a considerably more conservative outlook. She had four brothers—three older and one younger. Her younger brother, Robert, died on his motorcycle returning from World War II. That happened before I was born. My mother always told me that he was the sensitive one in the family. He was a poet and, like my mother, a musician. My younger brother, Robert, was named after him.

Mom studied music but did not pursue it as a career. My assumption is that she began playing the piano at the age of four. She fell in love with it. But music became her albatross, and the piano was her albatross, because she wasn't authorised or able to pursue it professionally. It became a symbol of what she couldn't do. No one in her family urged her to pursue it seriously. I won't suggest that her inability to pursue a profession in music caused or influenced her mental illness because I believe the majority of it was biological. But she suffered greatly as a result of her inability to pursue a musical career. It impacted her confidence, or lack thereof.

Later in life, my father told me that my mother was sexually raped in horrible ways by her father and one or more of her older brothers on multiple occasions as a child. My sister, Karyn, who had previously attended therapy sessions with my mother, later verified this to me.

3

Karyn kept this from me for years, and I don't think she made the wrong decision. Learning about this was unimaginably horrifying and heartbreaking, and I'm still trying to digest it.

I remember my mother being happy and us being happy together. She had an excellent sense of humour. We would giggle at all kinds of stuff. She would, however, wander in and out of her condition, as Sylvia Plath had. My father informed me she was previously diagnosed with manic depression and paranoid schizophrenia. They did not have the same medication as we do now.

I was born on January 26, 1953, in Lake Charles, Louisiana. You could say I was born to fight. Like most people, I don't remember my early years clearly, but my father constantly told me that I had to fight from the start. I was born with spina bifida, which is obviously not the best condition for someone who will spend a couple of hours every night standing on a platform, but I've conquered it just well. As a young child, I was frequently unwell. When I was about a year old, my windpipe got obstructed, necessitating an emergency tracheotomy. My father told me it was a close call, but I made it. I still have a noticeable scar from that treatment, and every time I look in the mirror, it reminds me of my challenging beginning and the possibility of growing stronger. My difficulties persisted for another couple of years. At one point, I contracted croup and had to be hospitalised in one of those oxygen humidity tents, after which I was quarantined at home in another oxygen tent in my bedroom.

After I was born, my parents' relationship deteriorated, and my father always claimed that I had it the worst. I was their first child, and the responsibilities brought a slew of new anxieties and tensions. When I was very little, my mother would get into these nasty moods, and no one knew what caused or prompted them. Two years later, my brother Robert was born, followed by my sister Karyn.

My mother used to tell me stories about how poor we were as babies and toddlers. She said that she had to borrow bread from the neighbours to feed us. They didn't have a crib for me, so my mother took a drawer from my chest and made it into my bed. Poverty exacerbated my parents' already strained relationship.

I am seventy years old, and I am still going through a lot of this. I've avoided discussing my childhood for decades, instead writing songs about it, since I believe I came to accept it as normal. "Okay, my mother is freaking out and yelling; my dad is in a bad mood today." I could tell everyone was trying. That seemed typical, the attempt.

I still recall one of my favourite photos of my father and me. I'm approximately two years old. We're standing on the front steps of our house, and it appears like we were getting ready to go to church or had just returned from church, because he's wearing a suit and I'm wearing a small dress and jacket. It's simply so lovely and innocent. We're just on the front stairs together. You can see we had a special bond. I had been so unwell, and by the time I was born, my mother's mental condition had begun to manifest itself, so my father was increasingly responsible for me.

Now that I've read numerous psychology books and undergone considerable therapy and self-education on mental illness and dysfunctional families, I know that I had no method of recognizing or dealing with the trauma that occurred to me. Kids will ultimately blame themselves. All of that energy goes somewhere. You are the tiny kid sitting in the locked closet, thinking and feeling, "What did I do wrong?" But then my father said, "It's not her fault, she's not well, you can't be angry at your mother." What was I going to do with all of my misery, bewilderment, and anger?

When I was eight years old and had just moved to Baton Rouge, I was referred to a child therapist. I dimly recall sitting in a room with this woman, playing some type of board game. My father expressed anxiety that I could be affected by my mother's illness. I don't believe I was acting out or anything. It was simply an issue of precaution. "We need to make sure everything's good," he told me. Perhaps my mother was going through a difficult time, and he was concerned that I would be scarred as a result.My father was a chemist, then a poet— not your conventional career path—and was constantly looking for teaching employment. He didn't get a permanent teaching position until I was 18 years old. We had moved twelve times since my birth. I remember nine of them. They believe that moving is one of the most stressful experiences in life. I moved twelve times before I was eighteen.

I've always felt comfortable on the road, moving around to advance my career. It's in my bloodstream. I feel at ease on buses and in hotels, and then I stand in front of people, almost like a travelling preacher, and communicate what I believe in the most, which is my music. And because most of my music is about my life, it's like a never-ending story that is lived, narrated, written, and sung.

When I was travelling with Bonnie Raitt in Vancouver in July 2022, my tour manager approached me one night and mentioned that there was an old man who would like to speak with me. Don Todd was a retired philosophy professor from Simon Fraser University. He was about 92 years old. He was dressed similarly to my father, in tan slacks and a button-down shirt, resembling a professor.

He had known my father growing up and told me stories about him and my grandfather. He informed me that my grandfather came from a small hamlet, a village, in the rural mountains of northern Arkansas. There were no roads or cars there; only mountain routes. There was a little, one-teacher school with six grades. My grandfather's education ended at sixth grade, thus he was still in his late teens with only that level of education. Until then, I had no idea my grandfather lived so far out in the wilderness, deep in the mountains.When I say, "I'm a southerner," many people think, "That must mean you're racist, you're this, you're that." There are numerous stereotypes linked with being Southern, which is a major issue in and of itself. That, I believe, is why my father taught me, "We are southerners, and we must fight those who believe that all southerners are racist, hicks, and stupid." That is how I was raised. That's my south.

One of my father's favourite anecdotes was about meeting Hank Williams a few months before my birth, in January 1953. He went to watch Hank play a show directly near Lake Charles, where my parents lived. He was bound and determined to meet him later. My father admired Hank and his music, and I believe that, aside from the similar surname, he simply felt a connection with him. They also appeared similar: tall, lanky, and gangly, with prominent cheekbones. It appears that they may have been linked.

After Hank's act, my father approached and introduced himself, and they ended up at a bar near the venue that Hank recommended. It was a gas station that offered alcohol; such establishments were common at the time. My father informed me that he and Hank were talking about how they didn't have any money growing up. He informed Hank that he was from Arkansas, grew up in a humble working-class household, and that his father was a Methodist preacher. He was now a poet and beatnik college lecturer. At some point, Hank asked my father what he wanted to drink, and my father requested bourbon and water. Hank's response: "Williams, you ought to be drinking beer 'cuz you got a beer-drinkin' soul."

Hank meant that, despite having a college education and becoming a professor, my father remained connected to the working-class environment. My father would retell this story over and over. It may have been the most essential lesson he ever taught me: being able to accept and move in both the world you were born into and the world you discovered on your own.

Hank died shortly afterward, and I was born three and a half weeks later.

Chapter 2

When I was about nine years old and we were living in Baton Rouge, my mother had a terrible mental breakdown and yelled at my father. This was not long after her strong support for John Ciardi at the reading. You can see how her mental instability made her unpredictable: anything may happen at any time, whether lovely or horrific. One day, she was pleasant and gorgeous in her jeans and a floral shirt that buttoned at the front, her hair nicely done. Then the next day, she would spiral out of control, looking like a shambles. Following the breakdown, I recall an ambulance arriving and transporting my mother. I tried to peep through the blinds to see what was going on. This woman, I believe one of our neighbours, had come into the house to look after us while my parents were away, and she said, "Don't look. "There is no reason to look." That made me extremely angry. If I want to look, I should be able to. I didn't want anyone to tell me what I could and couldn't do at the moment, especially someone I didn't know. You cannot see unless you can look.

When my parents split up, my mother asked if I wanted to stay with her or my father. I don't recall responding. I probably wanted to stay with my father. But I recall going into their closet and stroking their clothing individually—my mother's outfits and my father's shirts. That was all I could do at the time, and it somehow offered me comfort.

I can't fathom how difficult all of this was for my father, who was just 22 years old when I was born. His wife was unable to be a dependable mother to his ailing daughter.

He and I have a great bond. I believe I survived because of my closeness with him.

Yes, my family was dysfunctional and fucked up. But that's not what's important to me. What counts is that I got my father's writing aptitude and my mother's musical talent. My stepmother showed me how to prepare a table with cloth napkins and cutlery for a dinner party. Grandma Day also showed me how to make plant fertiliser by blending coffee grinds and eggshells, as well as how banana pudding and fig pickles should taste. Momma taught me religious hymns, and

Papaw taught me respect and diplomacy. In a way, my family was fantastic. Grandma Day crocheted pillowcases, and my aunt Alexa (on my father's side) kept note of every family member's birthday and always sent a card, along with one of her woven pot holders.

During those years, as my mother's mental illness progressed, I spent a lot of time at Uncle Bob and Aunt Alexa's residence. My cousin Mac would spend the night at a friend's place, while I slept in his bed. My father would leave me off there, then take my brother, Robert, to Grandma Day's place. She reportedly spoiled Robert.

My uncle Bob was a part-time performer who performed in a variety of plays and musicals at the Baton Rouge Little Theater. He arranged for me to play a small role in a local production of Annie Get Your Gun, a popular musical for provincial theatres in the 1960s. I fell in love with the stage throughout that performance. It was a year or two before I began playing guitar. Being in front of an audience with other cast members, including my cousin Mac, Uncle Bob's son, gave me a high I had never felt before. I was hooked. Bob was usually playing musical soundtracks on his stereo at home, too. I recall Oklahoma!, South Pacific, and others.

One of my first musical memories is of an outing my father took us on to get us out of the home while my mother was in a downward spiral. We lived in Macon, Georgia, and I was around five years old. Downtown Macon looked similar to many southern downtowns at the time, and it probably still does now. There was a broad main street with side streets, and the town was separated into two sections: white and black. There were massive antebellum houses on the white side of downtown. There was a dime store, barbershop, and soda shop. Consider the town square from the film Back to the Future, which is set around this time.

Blind Pearly Brown was a preacher and street singer in Macon. I'm not sure if my father knew him or if we just happened upon him while he was taking me to get ice cream or something. Brown was on the sidewalk, playing his guitar, singing, and collecting tips. I stood there, gripping my father's hand. It was an experience I'd never forget. I enjoyed the music so much that a few years later, my father purchased an album of songs recorded by folklorist Harry Oster. When I received my first guitar, the songs on that album were among the first I learnt. Songs like "God Don't Ever Change" and "You're Gonna Need That Pure Religion," which I hadn't realised were traditional.

Years later, I conducted research on Blind Pearly Brown. A reporter cited him in 1958 as stating, "I pray to the Lord that we will someday see a world without strife, where we can all live as brothers." I hope the Lord allows me to live to witness the day when people are considerate of one another. In another piece from 1972, Brown was reported as saying, "It's not horrible being a street singer. It'll teach you something. You should consider how certain people can be cruel to you."

To me, this is the core of the blues. It's about coming to terms with your experiences and learning from them.

Spending time with my mother's family exposed me to that kind of southern gothic experience, which I believe is why I adored Flannery O'Connor's writing. I first read her when I was sixteen, long after that visit, and was too young to appreciate her work. At sixteen, however, I discovered something that felt authentic. I started reading her short stories and devoured them all. I immediately realised what she was talking about.

There was a state mental hospital in Milledgeville, and the patients would wander around the town. Flannery was not an elitist. What she was talking about was also right in my backyard. It wasn't unusual for me. The southern gothic was my daily life.

When I first started performing this song in public, my father came to one of my gigs at the Bluebird in Nashville. It was his first time hearing the music. He approached me thereafter, dressed in his typical college professor pants, shirt and tie, and sport coat, thin as always, with his beard and glasses. He said, "I'm very sorry. "I'm so sorry." I asked him what he meant, and he explained, "That little girl crying in the backseat was you." It was a bittersweet moment that I will never forget. I was simultaneously amazed and moved. I didn't realise I was writing about myself the entire time! It took a poet to teach me.

I often wish I was more intellectually savvy in my lyrics, like Bob Dylan is. But all I can do is write about my own and other people's feelings, and I believe this is what distinguishes my music. It incorporates southern gothic themes, blues, folk, and rock.

I believe that if you delve deeply into things and are actually able to see, you can be wise and soulful. You don't need a formal education to be successful in whatever you do. I had numerous discussions about this with my father. He never made me feel awful for not loving a given writer or artist. For example, I've never liked Faulkner. I tried reading him, but I didn't like him. I prefer Flannery O'Connor and Carson McCullers. I was hesitant to inform my father because Faulkner was highly regarded at the time. I finally informed him, and he answered, "Oh, that's fine. You can read someone else. There are plenty of writers out there. "You don't have to like them all." Then he hesitated for a bit and said, "Plus, Faulkner was an asshole."

Chapter 3

My family and I relocated to Santiago, Chile, for a year in 1964, when I was eleven. A few years later, when I was seventeen, we spent a year in Mexico City, and these two years immersed in Latino cultures left an impression on me that continues to this day.

We went to Santiago because my father had been awarded an Amy Lowell Travelling Scholarship in Poetry. He met and befriended the renowned Chilean poets Pablo Neruda and Nicanor Parra. My father was buying Chilean music and listening to the local radio. Nicanor became a good friend of my father, and his sister was a famous musician named Violeta Parra, best known in America for her song "Gracias a la vida," which Joan Baez recorded years later. Violeta sang and played acoustic guitar in Chilean folk music, but her influence reached far beyond the country. By the time we came to Santiago, she had already recorded many albums, which Nicanor gave to my father. A documentary video dubbed her "the mother of Latin American folk music."

Her songs left a strong influence on me. Here was a woman in her forties, playing guitar and singing folk songs wonderfully and strongly. Joan Baez was the only American lady I was aware of at the time who worked in that capacity.

I had to wear a uniform to school and loathed it at first. But that rapidly changed as I fell in love with the location, culture, and music. Chile was experiencing political turmoil at the time, but I didn't completely understand what was going on until years later when we left. Many neighbouring nations were experiencing revolutions, but the turbulence in Chile was just getting started, with bloodshed rising over the next few years, eventually leading to Allende's overthrow in 1973. Víctor Jara, a singer-songwriter and activist, was seized by execution squads. His fingers were severed before he was slain. It was one of the most horrifying things I'd ever heard.

After my father's fellowship year in Santiago, we returned to Baton Rouge. I was fast getting into problems. In Chile, all of the girls wore tight-fitting slacks with no skirts. I owned several pairs of those pants, but when I wore them to school in Baton Rouge, I was instructed to go home and change because they were too tight. The principals and instructors thought such pants were naughty. In Santiago, everything was fine.

Jordan, my future stepmother, was introduced to my father during his first year back in Baton Rouge. She was an undergraduate in one of his LSU classes. He was thirty-five, and she was eighteen or nineteen. I was twelve. My sister Karyn was eight, and my brother Robert was ten.

Jordan was so young, she wasn't mature enough to manage the circumstances. A couple of my therapists have told me throughout the years that they believe I have a lot of unspoken animosity toward my father about what happened to Jordan, but I didn't express it because I didn't want to rock the boat. Children don't grasp how they feel. What did I do wrong? Who should I be furious at? I was stuck and perplexed.

My obsessive-compulsive disorder began the same year Jordan entered our home. That was when I started picking at my skin. Adolescent hormones were most likely starting to kick in as well. I was not a cutter, as Dusty Springfield portrayed herself in her memoirs, but I did cause some wounds and blisters.

In 1965, I purchased my first guitar and began taking lessons on it. I cannot overstate how volatile that year was for me. I was on the verge of becoming a teenager, with everything that entails for any girl, and Jordan was now a member of the family; I was experiencing a stew of emotions and desires. My teacher in Baton Rouge was a guitarist who also played in a rock band. Years later, as an adult, I couldn't recall his name, but I did have a photo of him. When I was researching this book, I shared that photo on social media, and some friends and admirers helped me find him. His name is Alan Jokinen, and he now resides in San Francisco. In Baton Rouge, he was a graduate student in poetry at LSU who studied with my father. He studied poetry during the day and performed in rock bands at night.

Alan used to come over to our place about once a week. He had long blond hair and a rockstar style. He was a lovely, sensitive man. We sit in the living room, and I'd tell him what music I wanted to learn and he'd show me how to play it. He taught me the rolling fingerpicking approach that I still use today. When I started working

13

on this book, Alan told me that I had the notion to learn to play this method. He claimed I told him I wanted to play folk songs. The first song I learned was "Freight Train" by Elizabeth Cotten. She used a fingerpicking approach similar to Piedmont blues. I was fascinated by Peter, Paul, and Mary, so I learnt how to play "Puff the Magic Dragon." Alan demonstrated me chords and fingerpicking techniques for whatever song I wanted, and I spent the remainder of the week practising that song. Then I'd have another song ready for him to teach me the following week, and he'd show me how to play it. My goal was not to become an accomplished guitarist, but rather to learn to play songs so that I could sing them.During the fall semester of that year, another of my father's students visited the house. He strolled in, clutching a record, and exclaimed, "Oh my God, you need to be listening to this." He put it on the turntable. It was Bob Dylan's new album Highway 61 Revisited, which was released at the end of August 1965. It totally blew my head. I couldn't comprehend the words or the song titles: "Just Like Tom Thumb's Blues," "Queen Jane Approximately," and "Ballad of a Thin Man." What does that entail for a 12-year-old girl? It did not matter. It struck me like a bolt of lightning, and I can still feel it when I listen to that record today.

I had never heard Bob Dylan before, but I had heard Woody Guthrie and was familiar with the intellectual world of poetry thanks to my father. On this record, poetry abruptly gave way to badass rock and roll. Dylan had taken from all of these realms, bringing them together for the first time. I was utterly mesmerised. I really liked the record cover, which featured his hair and a strange figure holding a camera. That was it for me. Between that record and Joan Baez's little T-shirt, bare feet, and long hair, I knew I wanted to be knew I wanted to be a part of that world since I was twelve old.

fall in love with someone you have never met? It may not love, but it is certainly similar to it. Dylan has had a impact on many men and women, including myself. He ntor and musical partner. Of course, he was unaware of ut it didn't matter. I could have a dream. After hearing Revisited, I started listening to all of his other albums, ther Side of Bob Dylan and The Freewheelin' Bob my constant companion, or I was his shadow. I

14

wanted to be like him in some way. I wanted to do exactly what he was doing. "Blowin' in the Wind" and "Don't Think Twice, It's All Right" were among the first songs I learnt to play. Also, his song "To Ramona," which could be my favourite Dylan tune of all time. It's a love song for a woman. "Ramona come closer, shut softly your watery eyes." He could have stated "eyes," but instead says "watery eyes." That single word has a profound impact. It implies that the woman had cried or was about to cry. I also enjoy the melody and its Spanish flair.

As soon as I learned how to play the guitar, I spent much of my leisure time sitting around learning these tunes. I am still doing that today. From the age of twelve to seventy, I've been doing the same thing, and I enjoy it. It's the world I wished to live in, a better one than the one I was in.

Chapter 4

A year or a year and a half later, in 1966 or 1967, Dad accepted a teaching position at Loyola in New Orleans, and we packed up and relocated once more. I was 13 or 14 years old. My parents had split, and Jordan was about to become my stepmother. Mama also moved to New Orleans, but she had her own house. My sister, brother, and I stayed with my father and Jordan, but we made regular visits to my mother. At the time, I couldn't express how messed up and confusing things were for us kids. That was the only thing I knew. I guess when you grow up in a certain atmosphere, even if you know better, you tend to believe that everyone else lives the same way. However, your parents' divorce in the late 1960s was a significant event. Everyone would inquire, "Why do you live with your father? "How come you're not with your mother?" There was a sense of guilt associated with not living with your mother.

However, we arrived in New Orleans at the perfect time for me. It was the ideal setting for a teen who was passionate about music. In one of his songs, Neil Young states, "All my changes were there." He is talking about growing up in Canada. That is how I feel about my time in New Orleans between the ages of fourteen and sixteen. You can't fathom how much and what kind of music was filling my head. For this song to come to me at such an impressionable age, when my little girl's body and soul were beginning to change so dramatically, triggered a crazy mix of events in my head and heart, some strange, some good, and some possibly not so good.

In New Orleans, I had largely male pals, and we all loved music; it was our anchor. I did not find many girls that wanted to play music. I spent a lot of time at a house on Lowerline Street in Uptown, near Tulane, where two brothers, David and Cranston Clements, lived. I was dating Fielding Henderson, who played guitar in certain high school bands and introduced me to them. I believed they were significant because Fielding said so.

I listened to what he said. We adored each other and cared only about music and rescuing the world. We walked about New Orleans discussing current affairs, cultural tensions, and the latest album we had heard. We still had so much to learn. We were starving for knowledge. When Fielding introduced me to David and Cranston, I felt they were kindred spirits.

Sometimes we'd skip school to listen to a new record. Alternatively, we may ride the St. Charles streetcar into downtown. Weinstein's, a variety store, sold records, as did Smith's Record Center. When we had money, we would buy music. We'd hang around in the French Quarter. We were teens going around observing and taking everything in. There was an establishment called Buster Holmes' Bar and Restaurant. Clarence "Buster" Holmes was the unquestioned master of red beans and rice. Going there was considered a rite of passage for everyone growing up in New Orleans. David, Cranston, and I would find 75 cents and walk up to the take-out screen window at Buster's, where we would order three plates of red beans and rice for 25 cents each. We would sit on the sidewalk and eat.

One of my favourite memories from that time is my father taking us to Preservation Hall to watch a woman named Sweet Emma play the piano and sing. It gave me an idea of what it was like to listen to Memphis Minnie in the 1930s and 1940s. Sweet Emma sang unpolished jazz and blues songs. There was no air conditioning, so I'd sit there listening to her while sweating. Sweating through your clothes is common for New Orleans residents.

One night, there was a very large party at David and Cranston's house, and several black youngsters were hanging there. The crowd spilled out onto the front yard, and someone phoned the cops since there were black children present. The police arrived and shut down the party. When David and Cranston's father learned about it, he was outraged that his sons were hanging around with black children. He attempted to straighten them out. He pushed them to leave their mother's house and live with him and their stepmother. But it didn't stick. They rebelled. They were expelled from high school, and a friend of theirs stole his father's car, so they all left town, planning to drive to California. Each of them had saved his allowance for the vacation, but they still didn't have enough money to do much. They travelled as far as El Paso, Texas, before being apprehended by authorities after one of them stole a bottle of Coca-Cola from a petrol station.

I was booted out of high school twice for engaging in demonstrations. At the time, all the excellent schools in New Orleans were Catholic, but I attended a public school named Fortier, pronounced "for-shay," a French name that everyone mispronounced as "for-tee-er." It was in the Uptown neighbourhood of New Orleans, in a massive four-story brick-and-limestone structure with a stately main entrance of fifteen or twenty broad stairs leading to three double doors. There were so many steps that the school's entrance was on the second story. Inside, there were wooden floors and little metal lockers. It was overcrowded and understaffed, and although having recently been integrated, the principal was openly racist.

I was booted out for the first time before the bell rang one morning. A friend of mine asked if I would distribute fliers from Students for a Democratic Society around campus. SDS leaflets were lists of grievances and requests compiled by students. When a black kid and a white youngster got into a fight at school, the black kid was sent home but the white kid was not. We demanded that such uneven treatment stop. I was discovered handing out pamphlets and was sent to the assistant principal's office with two other students. The assistant principal admonished us and warned us not to do it again or we would be expelled from school.

I tried, I really did. But a few weeks later, when I arrived at school one morning, a massive anti-racism rally was underway, with a large march around the school. The NAACP was present, and SDS joined in. I was in my homeroom, watching the march from the window. Some of the students in my class were spitting out the window at the demonstrators. Teenagers in New Orleans back then were just as split as their parents. Two progressive friends of mine noticed me at the window and cried, "Come on down!" I couldn't resist. My blood was racing, and I was thinking, "I gotta go down there." So I raced out of my homeroom to join the march. The officers arrived and began tossing people into paddy trucks. I was able to escape and make it back home.

More than fifty years later, I'm still in touch with David and Cranston. When I'm in New Orleans, my husband, Tom, and I will visit with them. David eventually opened a club called Snake and Jake's Christmas Club Lounge, which is now one of New Orleans' most well-known dive bars. David opened this pub in part to recreate the old free-form house party of his boyhood. Cranston became a highly accomplished guitarist, performing with everyone in New Orleans over the years, including Dr. John, the Nevilles, and Irma Thomas. It's funny to me that the three of us were such jerks as teenagers, and yet we've all gotten jobs doing something we enjoy.

Mama was always able to find these great enormous old New Orleans flats. One location was on Carrollton Avenue, near St. Charles. It was easily accessible because the streetcar stopped directly at the corner. She always kept her apartments cosy and comfy. She enjoyed folk art from several nations and had some from when we were in Santiago. She had a tremendous record collection, and I helped her add to it. One of her favourite records was Erroll Garner's Concert by the Sea. She accumulated a large collection of sheet music, which she stored in her piano bench and on top of the piano. The sheet music seemed like a fantastic mystery to me.

I felt good about being able to aid her in her later years when my finances improved. A year ago, I assisted her in purchasing a vehicle. Her health eventually deteriorated, and I had to assist her in moving into an assisted living facility I discovered in Fayetteville, Arkansas, which she came to enjoy. Robert and Karyn were present, along with Dad and Mama Jordan, to keep an eye on her. Dad and Mama Jordan never abandoned my mother. I admire this about them. Whatever wrongdoing had occurred was always forgiven.

Chapter 5

In 1970, my family packed up and relocated to Mexico City for a year. My father held a fellowship at one of the universities there. We rented a two-story yellow house in the Distrito Federal section of town. The house came with a housekeeper who lived in the back with her daughter. I would have been a junior, but I was not accepted into the high school. If I recall correctly, I was denied admission to school because I was unable to gather my proper papers after getting expelled from high school in New Orleans.

Trouble broke out during political demonstrations in Mexico City about a year before we arrived there. The marchers had been granted permission by the government to protest, but the military and police surrounded them and opened fire. People were either slain or dragged away. During our year there, we met many folks who had friends or relatives who were missing and had no idea what had happened to them. That seemed alarming to me.

There was a small park not far from our house where I met several of the younger hippie-type people. I would hang out with them and smoke marijuana. They were always trying to get me to go to Oaxaca for the mushrooms. I met one attractive Mexican guy who didn't speak English, so we exclusively spoke in Spanish. He continued telling me things like "tener sexo" and "quiero tener sexo." I hadn't had sex yet, and my father was frightened that I would become pregnant or that I would be arrested for smoking marijuana, causing him to lose his fellowship and us all to be deported. But happily, none of those occurred.

The politically leftist, younger, progressive liberals in Mexico City were anti-American as a result of Vietnam, so we had to work hard to break down that instinctual barrier in order to make friends with them. People who weren't anti-American were stiff and conservative, not our kind, so we couldn't have the literary house parties my father used to throw. It was different from Santiago, where we had met numerous poets and writers. We invited all of our friends from the United States to visit us during our year in Mexico, and the majority of them did.

My mother was unable to visit, but I remained in regular contact with her by mail and phone. In New Orleans, she worked in an insurance company's office doing clerical labour, primarily answering phones. People would phone with policy questions, and she would talk to them for hours, becoming friends with the company's clients and consumers. I'd phone her from Mexico and she'd tell me about all the individuals she'd spoken with, or she'd write me notes. Because she worked in insurance, she heard a lot of stories of what happened to families from various walks of life, such as accidents, fires, and seniors losing their pensions. She appreciated hearing the stories and attempting to help others; perhaps it alleviated her own grief.

When Clark was there, my father had invited two people from the American embassy to join us. Clark and I were performing folk songs when one of those two people suggested, "We should send Cindy"—yes, I was called Cindy at the time—"and Clark out on the road to play some shows around Mexico."

It turned out to be an unforgettable experience for me. The embassy and the US Information Agency organised thirty performances across the country for us. We packed Clark's car and went around Mexico, staying in hotels designated for us by the embassy. We generally played traditional American folk tunes in high schools and universities, as well as songs by Dylan, Peter, Paul, and Mary. The government officials believed it was a way to spread American goodwill throughout Mexico at a time when America was not popular, and that it would show the Mexican people that America was more than just bombs and the military, and that we had a folk cultural tradition similar to theirs. The embassy described our performance as "Folk Music from Spiritual to Protest with Clark Jones and Cindy Williams."

This was my first time playing live gigs in front of strangers, and it was both nerve-racking and exciting. Between the ages of twelve and seventeen, I spent much of my time playing guitar alone or in a living room with friends and family. Now I was standing in front of a large audience, sometimes with Clark in a duo, sometimes alone.

I recall playing a couple performances in San Miguel de Allende, a picturesque artist's colony. The audience included painters, artisans, musicians, and writers. I was astounded by how beautifully we were handled. After the show, I was given a bunch of flowers.

The embassy promoted the tour heavily, and there was considerable media coverage.

When I reflect back on my life, I realise that I've had a number of guardian-angel-like characters that softly but firmly guided me through my trade and career. Clark was among the first of these figures. He was a gorgeous person with a large, warm heart. I was supposed to be in high school, but instead I was travelling over Mexico with Clark, playing folk music. It was an education that no school could have provided me.

Chapter 6

I missed Woodstock. I just missed the Haight-Ashbury event in San Francisco. I missed the folk era in Greenwich Village, New York. I knew about them, but I was too young to pack my belongings and travel to any of these locations to participate.

But I did get to see a wonderful literary setting. Most summers in the 1960s, we would travel to Middlebury, Vermont, for the Bread Loaf Writers' Conference, which is similar to the Woodstock of writers' conferences. For a period, John Ciardi directed it, and he brought my father on board as a faculty member. All of the student authors resided in these historic dorms, while the instructors and their families stayed in log cabins down the road in a rural region away from the main campus. Throughout the day, there were sessions where younger writers' work was assessed, followed by free time to work in the afternoon. In the evenings, everyone gathered at the Barn, a large ancient building with a massive fireplace. In between readings by known writers, there was essentially one big party where everyone drank and celebrated together. Younger writers had to go through a rigorous application process before being welcomed to Bread Loaf. It was a major occasion for them, as well as for me, who was sixteen or seventeen and had just graduated from a rigorous high school in New Orleans. Being at Bread Loaf was a higher level of something, but I'm sure I couldn't have specified what.

During those years, I became interested in several poets. One year, I got extremely interested in a poet named John, who had blond hair. We spent some time together during the nighttime celebration hours. Nothing transpired between us save long discussions about music and literature, which were significant to me. We stayed in touch through letters, and we'd meet again at Bread Loaf the following summer. He was calm and sensitive, a highly artistic kind.

Those summers at Bread Loaf were wonderful, but something terrible happened to me during one visit. I was sixteen or seventeen. I believe it was 1970 when we visited Mexico, returned to the United States for Bread Loaf, and then returned to Mexico.

Another time, in my twenties, I was driving down the interstate and my car broke down. A man was going toward me, and at first I assumed he was coming to help, but as he approached, I noticed he had a massive erection protruding out of his pants. I jumped in the car and shut the doors. He just stood there with this erection outside my window, asking if I needed assistance. Finally, he departed.

These occurrences left me traumatised. A mark or wound was inflicted upon me. I was left feeling a little more terrified and distrustful. However, it pales in contrast to what my mother went through. Now that I know more about what happened to her as a child, I'm astonished she handled it so well.

When I was thirty-one years old and had moved to Los Angeles, I decided to go up to San Francisco, where I planned to try to find Charles Bukowski. I enjoyed his writing, and I had recently moved to California, so it seemed logical for me to do. When I told my father about it, he replied, "Well, honey, you know that he'll probably try to screw you." Nobody uses the phrase anymore. What number of fathers would say that to their 31-year-old daughter?

When I go back to my late teens and those literary workshops and parties at our house, I remember that my father was in his forties and Jordan was probably twenty-three or twenty-four years old. My father must have been proud. He has this youthful arm candy while holding all of these literati parties. Many of those male writers were hunting for it back then, even if they were married. Maybe they still do it now.

One aspect of my life that I believe stemmed from my involvement in this chaotic atmosphere as a teenager was a lack of desire to have my own children. Never. It was not a difficult decision for me, and I have no regrets today. I went on birth control at the age of eighteen, and it never occurred to me to become a mother. Not once. Growing up, I never saw any families truly enjoying their children. I recall thinking as a teenager, "Wow, no one seems to enjoy having children. Nobody appears to be happy about having children. "It is a burden, not a joy." Everyone seemed to want to party and fuck each other freely. Family commitments and responsibilities did not appear to be the most important thing for anyone, so why should they have been essential to me?

Nowadays, I look around and am depressed when I see pregnant ladies or parents with young children because I wonder, "Will this child have a good upbringing? Are these kids going to get a good education? Will these youngsters have excellent parents? I do not know. I make no judgments about it. It's simply a feeling about the difficulties of fatherhood that I began to have in my late teens, based on my personal experiences.

My father and stepmother's residence was constantly visited by intriguing guests. I like that environment, and after leaving home and living on my own, I began to regret it greatly. I tried to recreate it myself, but I was never successful, even with all of the musicians I knew. I missed the literary world, the stimulating conversations, the cocktails, the wit, the warmth, the astuteness, and the beauty.

Dad also began a poetry workshop in the Cummins Unit jail in Gould, Arkansas. Another writer, Bob Ward, paid us a visit one day, and Dad invited Bob and me to accompany him on one of his journeys to the prison. I took my guitar and performed for the female convicts of the women's facility. It was a terrible prison where they would eventually carry out executions. Needless to say, it was a memorable event.

Even though I never finished high school, my father was able to get me into the University of Arkansas, where I enrolled after we returned from Mexico. However, it did not take. I hardly lasted a semester. During the Christmas break between semesters, I travelled to New Orleans to see my mother and decided to stay. I had discovered Andy's on Bourbon Street, which was looking for singer-songwriters to perform regular performances for tips. It was centrally located among the strip clubs and tourist attractions. It was just a stool with a few mics, and they were open all night until daybreak. Tourists would come in and check things out. Artists would sign up to play during specific time slots, such as 8:00 p.m. to midnight or 9:00 p.m. to 1:00 a.m. I auditioned and was assigned a regular time slot at Andy's. I was quite excited. My first regular gig. I played sets for a few weeks and earned decent money. It was enough to cover a month's rent, which was roughly $85.00 to share a room with someone back then. I was scheduled to return to university, but instead I called my father and told him about this employment. He went on: "Honey, if you want to stay and do that instead of going back to school, that's fine with me." I was quite thrilled. That remains a watershed moment in my life. What if my father had responded, "No, you have to return to college"?

I never felt at ease in that type of environment. But of course, I couldn't say anything because I'd be perceived as rigid and unfree. During those days, the concept of freedom spiralled out of control. Women were putting themselves in uncomfortable situations in the name of freedom. I knew what guys were capable of.

Soon later, a wonderful man named Zac joined my life. He was lanky and slender, with a full head of wavy blond hair and a huge grin. He was childlike in a charming way. We spent time together and had fun all over New Orleans, which made him even more special to me. He didn't project a macho attitude. He was all about love, peace, and beauty; he was a true hippie, not a chauvinist disguised as a hippie.

I had wanted to try LSD for a long time, but I had been told to wait until I was eighteen years old. After my birthday, Zac and I decided on a trip together. The acid was named orange sunshine. We spent much of our time in his room, with the windows open, music playing, and rolling around naked on his bed and a blanket on the floor. We were hallucinating, giggling, and playing with one another. We had no concerns in the world. I loved it. I had a copy of Ram Dass' book Be Here Now, which was popular at the time. I took that book everywhere I went, as if it were the Bible. I was on a spiritual journey. I was researching many routes and religions, with the exception of Christianity, which I couldn't connect with. It was possibly owing to my father's pragmatic viewpoints. Despite the fact that his father was a Methodist minister, he identified as an agnostic. It could become a little confusing.

Chapter 7

In 1972, I travelled to Nashville to audition at Opryland. My father's buddy, Tom T. Hall's bass player, arranged for me to come there and audition, as well as to stay for a short while.

One night at the Exit/In, I met this musician, and we asked him back to our place, where we sat around and played music while drinking Southern Comfort and smoking weed. The cops suddenly knocked on our door, and we replied, and they came in and began searching the entire house for weed, which they could obviously smell. They discovered someone's stash and a pot pipe in my room, so everyone was brought in, except Wrecks, who managed to escape. We got down to the station, and they eventually let everyone go except for myself and this guy named Skinny Dennis, so we spent the night in the county jail.

I recall the artist Rodney Crowell becoming involved in all of this as well; I believe he was about to move into the house, so he and a couple of the other residents were attempting to raise bail for us. We did leave the next day; one night in that place was sufficient for me. But by this point, my father was aware of what was going on—most likely because I wanted him to post bail. We hired Rose Palermo, a lawyer with a reputation for being "understanding" to musicians.

One of the disadvantages of growing up as the granddaughter of two church families was that I was always plagued by terrible personal guilt. So, on the one side, there's all this insane southern gothic things going on in the backdrop of my youth, but you still have southern Sunday church expectations to deal with. I didn't have a mother telling me what to do or what to wear when going out in public. My parents did not do that. But the rigorous, respectable church culture was always present. The strain of a specific ideal makes you feel extremely bad if, like me, you come nowhere close to achieving it.

And here I was, having never finished high school, attempting to be a professional musician in my twenties, and feeling like a fuckup most of the time. When you add in the 1960s and 1970s hippy culture, I struggled to find my place in society.

I believe that meeting some older blues musicians when I arrived in Austin in 1974 helped to release me from a lot of the exclusive and confining southern Christian guilt and hippie nonsense. I was dating Rich Layton when he was hired as the sound engineer for the Blues Caravan, a touring blues revue. Musicians included Pinetop Perkins, Furry Lewis, and Big Memphis Ma Rainey. I was invited to join them. I didn't participate; I simply tagged along.

At the time, I was beating myself up with all these guilty thoughts, some of which were true and some of which were exaggerated in my mind: "I'm staying out too late, drinking too much, smoking cigarettes, eating too much sugar, eating too much fried chicken and barbecue, fucking my neighbor's ex-boyfriend, fucking this guy or that guy who I shouldn't be fucking." I was dealing with a great deal of personal guilt. The blues advise you to embrace all of life, as in "I've worked my ass off and I'm going to enjoy myself and not feel guilty about it." Every time I started beating myself up for breaking the rules, I remembered those blues guys and how they weren't concerned with how much whiskey they were drinking, how much barbecue they were eating, how many cigarettes they'd had, or how many women they'd fucked. There is something to be said about that freedom.

I had been hanging out with Kurt Van Sickle, who had taken on the responsibility of managing Mance. Kurt was a singer and songwriter himself. He asked whether I wanted to go meet Mance. Of course, I replied, it would be an honour. I'd been listening to and learning from Mance's recordings for years. Kurt and I drove out to his house and picked up Mance at a bus stop. Mance was looking for something to eat, and he knew of a greasy spoon that served wonderful BBQ. So we paused at this dive.

Many of these blues musicians are adamant about which tunes they wrote but did not receive credit for. They do not tolerate fools well. Mance performed "Key to the Highway" for us, insisting that he wrote it in the 1920s or 1930s. Today, that music is deemed public domain and is not ascribed to anyone. Big Bill Broonzy's rendition was the first I heard, and of course, Eric Clapton popularised it as a rock song. When Duane Allman passed away, "Key to the Highway" was played during his funeral in Macon, Georgia. Mance insisted he wrote it. That night at his place, he performed a couple additional renowned songs that he said he wrote but was never given credit for. I believed him.

The next morning, Kurt and I awoke to Mance's wife preparing bacon, fried eggs, and fried potatoes on the stove. It was the kind of breakfast the hippies said you weren't meant to have. Granola and yoghurt were the hippy breakfast. I recall seeing Mance's wife prepare this breakfast for us and thinking about how the hippy lifestyle may be scary and restrictive in its own way. The blues musicians taught me to be irrepressible, or encouraged me to embrace my irrepressible streak.

I never finished high school, let alone college, yet I am aware that what I have written may be considered part of the "noble savage" attitude that is addressed in academia. I see it. The truth is that my pain was genuine, and I was processing my past traumas for the first time. I associated with the blues musicians. Their lack of pretence contrasted with much of the social literary environment I'd encountered and, to be honest, liked over the years. Being a blues musician also required a certain level of work ethic. You can't learn to play this song unless you spend a lot of time practising it. Mance had been playing these tunes all his life. He wasn't attempting to add something to his résumé or get accepted into anything. He was only performing the tunes he loved. That's all I wanted to do: play tunes I wanted to play.

Chapter 8

Throughout my adolescence in the late 1960s, my father was always strict with me about cigarettes, sex, and contraception. He informed me, "I understand that many kids are already having sex, but if you wait until you are eighteen, we will get you the pill. And don't smoke cigarettes. They're harmful for you." We had a little bargain, so that's what I did. I did not have sex till I was eighteen. However, once I began taking the tablet, I wasted little time. Those were the days when you'd just keep going and going till your bed broke or something. The beds were cheap back then, at least the ones we used when we were little. Some very amusing things happened on those inexpensive beds, and you'd say, "Oops." These were the days of unfettered love. I never took to cigarettes, and I'm so glad I didn't because not smoking has allowed my singing voice to mature and flourish throughout my life and career. I believe my singing is as strong as it has ever been. I don't sound like I did when I was younger; it's different, but as nice, in my opinion.

I've been described as an "erotic" songwriter. I do not disagree, however despite having a lot of sex when I was younger, I was never promiscuous. I've always had companions. Some of them didn't stay long, but I wasn't sleeping around randomly. For me, the brain is the true erogenous zone, thus I need to connect with someone intellectually and nearly spiritually before I can be physically attracted to them, which rarely happens right away. I realised early in my adult life that talking—real, honest, substantive conversation—could be superhot, and it didn't have to end with anyone taking their clothes off to be erotic in a long-term way, in a way that can last longer in your mind, memory, and feelings than physical sex. Often, a good discussion is more memorable than fucking. That's what I was trying to say with my song "Something About What Happens When We Talk" from the Sweet Old World album.

As I matured into a full-fledged woman, I became attracted to a specific type of male, and I would maintain that attraction for the rest of my adult life. I typically describe this kind of individual as "a poet on a motorcycle." These were men capable of deep thought and emotion, but they also had a blue-collar roughneck character. Frank

Stanford, the poet, was the embodiment of this kind of character in my opinion.

I met Frank around the spring of 1978. I was 25 years old at the time. I had been living in Houston and Austin, plying my trade and craft in those towns' music scenes and working odd jobs in restaurants and health food stores to pay my bills, but I was frequently returning to Fayetteville to see my father and Jordan (Momma J, as we came to call her), and I would sometimes stay for weeks or months at a time. Dad's literary gatherings continued as usual at the house, and I would occasionally get out my guitar and play songs in the evenings.

Frank had attended the University of Arkansas in Fayetteville and studied poetry in my father's department, but I do not believe he completed his degree. He was regarded as a legendary character in Fayetteville's literary circles, but he never became well-known outside of the town. My father encouraged Frank to focus on translating poetry from foreign languages, although I'm not sure if their professional relationship was particularly close. Frank had already published several volumes of poetry when I met him, but he was working as a land surveyor to make ends meet. I like a man who is both a land surveyor and a poet.

I found him irresistible, as did many other ladies and men. Everybody wanted to be near him. He was a cross between Jack Kerouac and a Southern country guy. He was stocky, highly fit, and built like a wrestler or a rodeo performer. He was simultaneously charismatic and intriguing, swashbuckling and sympathetic. When you look at images of him, you can see why ladies fell in love with him. He was charismatic and captivating, yet he also seemed tormented, brooding at times and unstable. He was married to another lady before Ginny, and I was informed he spent some time in a psychiatric hospital following their divorce.

I was enamoured and in love with him. I'm not sure what you'd call our relationship. I wouldn't call it a love triangle or square with me, Ginny, and Carolyn because Frank and I never had sex. We simply hung out and talked. He actually listened to what I had to say and knew precisely what to say in return. He understood what I wanted to hear, which implies manipulation, but it also indicates that he cared. We talked about poetry and lyrics and feelings and desires, all sorts of topics about caring about individuals and caring for the world, about how the world was fucked up and so hard on most people while some people had it easy, and why it was important to be a poet or a singer even if your audience was never going to be large, as it appeared to be for me at the time.

Frank and I dated for about two months before he committed suicide by shooting himself in the chest with a revolver. There are several tales of what led to his suicide.

Essentially, all of the stories agree that Ginny and Carolyn had had enough of Frank's philandering and faced him simultaneously, almost as an intervention, and he couldn't take it. He had been out of town for a few weeks before this incident. He might have gone to New Orleans to see the poet Ellen Gilchrist, with whom he was friendly. He was often leaving town for what he said were land surveying tasks, but Ginny and Carolyn discovered that he was having affairs with women all across the region. When he arrived from this specific excursion, he discovered Ginny and Carolyn waiting for him. They informed him that they had discovered his game and that he needed to choose one of them and stay with it, or they would both leave him. He went down the street to a friend's house, borrowed a weapon, and then returned to the house to shoot himself. The entire incident resembled a Shakespearean tragedy.

I was playing a gig in Dallas not long after Frank's death, and his sister, Ruth, attended and made her way backstage afterward. She had yet another perspective on Frank's demise. "I have no regard or respect for Ginny or Carolyn," I heard her say. She assumed they knew what they were getting into when they became connected with Frank. She believed they had ambushed him. When Frank returned from his trip, he found his truck covered in women's underwear, including bras, panties, and lingerie. She felt they should have realised that what they did would humiliate and crush him. They knew he had spent time in a mental hospital following his first divorce. They weren't wrong to approach him, but they didn't have to be so dramatic. Anyway, it is her version. Perhaps she was being the protective sister.

Frank sent me flowers to my father's house, and they came on the day he committed suicide. I'm not sure if he sent them on the same day, the day before, or what. I received the flowers, but I never saw him alive again. He had sent the flowers to let me know he was thinking of me while he was away.

The element of Frank's burial that still haunts me today, as depicted in "Pineola," is that there was a large turnout of his friends and followers, yet his family knew none of them, and vice versa. At Frank's tomb, two people from different worlds met for the first and only time. I can't let go of that image.

I did pick up some soil and throw it on the gravesite. It was a southern Gothic story. A girl stood there with a tiny secret. There I was, with Ginny, Carolyn, Frank's mother, and sister all present, and I was the only one who knew how I felt about Frank. Later, I learned that Ginny and Carolyn lived together for a period after Frank died. Another dark twist in the plot.

After my song was released and I became more well-known in my career, Frank Stanford's legend grew. New editions of his books have been published. People began researching him and his work. Some people say my music sparked Frank's interest, but I'm not sure. It could have been a coincidence. A writer phoned me once, maybe thirty or thirty-five years after Frank died, and said he had been looking through Frank's papers at Yale University and found my name in them. He informed me that Frank wrote: "I feel free." I've been hanging out with Lucinda, and she makes me feel freer." That made me feel fantastic, but it was also somewhat unnerving. This writer implied that Frank and I had a stormy affair, which is not accurate.

Chapter 9

When I was residing in New Orleans in 1972, I met another singer-songwriter named Jeff Ampolsk, which laid the groundwork for my Folkways record deal. We remained in touch, and a few years later, he recorded an album for Folkways. I was aware of Mo Asch's iconic label, which is now part of the Smithsonian, but I never imagined I'd be able to record with them. In early 1978, Jeff and I were conversing, and he told me, "If you send a cassette demo to Mo, I bet he will make a record for you."

I was sceptical, but Jeff persuaded me to do it and gave me the address. I prepared a cassette of the songs I'd been playing at performances and gave it to Mo. These songs were renditions of classics by artists such as Robert Johnson, Memphis Minnie, Hank Williams, and Sleepy John Estes.

Sure enough, a few weeks later, Mo offered to give me $300 for a record. It was that simple. My first record deal was with a label that had produced a lot of music I adored, including old folk and traditional pieces that I had been listening to since I was a child. Now I just needed to find a studio where I could record.

I signed my one-page contract with Folkways, and I decided it was only fitting that I come to New York City to meet the great Mo (short for "Moses") Asch. He turned out to be really pleasant, albeit in a hard-boiled New Yorker way. Despite his tough exterior, he had a good-natured grandfatherly demeanour about him. I had the utmost regard for him and what he had accomplished with the label. Folkways was to folk music what Blue Note was to jazz: legendary and admired. It was a huge deal for me to be recognized by Mo and Folkways. I knew they couldn't make me a star, but that didn't bother me at all. I would join an artist family, and I was confident that the label would look after me.

Tom was one of these "guardian angels" who assisted me at critical junctures in my career. When he learned about Folkways' offer, he called me and said, "I know a guy who works as an engineer at Malaco Studios in Jackson. I helped him get out of a narcotics charge, so he owes me a favour. Why don't I see if I can schedule some studio time for you at Malaco, and you can come here to record and stay at my house?"

Malaco was a renowned R&B and blues studio. Musicians such as Bobby "Blue" Bland and Little Milton have recorded there. (Unfortunately, it was destroyed by a tornado in 2011.) I invited a guitarist from Houston, John Grimaudo, and we slept at Tom's place and cut the record in one afternoon. We recorded classic covers that I had been doing for years. That's what was on my demo cassette, and I assumed that was what Folkways would want.

John returned to Houston, and I ended up residing at Tom's house for several months in the fall of 1978. He greeted me and even let me use his MG sports car. I recall walking into his house one day and seeing Tom sitting alone in the kitchen, eating boiled peanuts and boiled eggs. He was following an Atkins diet. He was quite friendly to me.

I played gigs anywhere I could in Jackson, and I met Franck Madoeuf, a Frenchman who taught French at a local ladies' school. The inaugural Delta Blues Festival took place in Greenville, Mississippi, over the course of one weekend in October of that year. I drove to the event with Franck. Furry Lewis and Bukka White were among the artists performing. Franck and I went about the event both together and individually before meeting back at the car to go back to Jackson. While strolling, I came across this young man with a guitar. He was from Greenville and appeared young, although he was already a Vietnam veteran. He was one of those lonely, road-weary sorts who I gravitate toward. He told me that the battle had left him scarred. In today's standards, I believe he would be classified as having PTSD. We spent the day listening to music and chatting. Something about him made an effect on me. I never met him again, but we stayed in touch by correspondence for a time. The next day, I began writing notes for "Greenville," a song that would be released twenty years later on Car Wheels on a Gravel Road.

My Folkways CD was published later, in 1979, and I decided that the best thing I could do was relocate to New York City. I lived there for approximately eight months, which was about all I could take. It was difficult to be there while I was broke. By the time I arrived in the city, the exciting folk scene I'd always read about—when Bob Dylan and Joan Baez were hanging out in coffeehouses and dreams were being made—had mostly faded, though some of the legendary venues remained open. There were also several fantastic aspiring singer-songwriters in attendance. Suzanne Vega's performances blew everyone away. She was a beautiful girl with intriguing eyes and a mystery about her. She drew you into her orbit. Her approach to a song was striking: she had perfected the art of cheap and efficient songwriting—clean and without frills, no vibrato.

One night, after finishing my show at Folk City, I strolled off stage and into the crowd, heading toward the bar. Mike approached me and said, "Loooo-cinda, I want you to meet a friend of mine."

"Of course," I responded.

Then he turned back to face the bar and pointed to a skinny, unnoticeable man sitting on a barstool. As we approached, Mike introduced himself as Bobby Dylan.

I extended my hand without thinking, but then I recognized what was going on and froze. My idol stood directly in front of me, looking at me. Let me just say that I felt the blood surge through my body, through my heart, and into my head. I received the impression that there was no one else in the room save Dylan. It is difficult to convey because it is unlike anything I have felt before or subsequently. The kinetic energy was tangible. He eventually had to leave since, like Bob Dylan, he couldn't keep hanging out. I chose to stand near the door so that when he left, he would see me. As he moved to the door, he bent over and gently kissed the side of my face. He told me, "Let's keep in touch. We'll be heading on the road again soon." I was in heaven. I walked on air back to my East Village flat.

Two decades later, Dylan's management approached me about opening gigs for him and Van Morrison on a tour they were planning together. "Hell yeah, I'll do that," I replied. We performed a couple months of gigs together, but I never had the opportunity to chat with Bob or Van the entire time. Perhaps it is better that way. I remember that lovely night.

Chapter 10

Another guardian angel figure that appeared in my life was Hobart Taylor, whom I still consider a dear friend. I met him in 1976, two years before my Folkways contract, while I was living in Houston and performing at Anderson Fair and other venues in Houston and Austin. Lyle Lovett and Nanci Griffith performed at Anderson Fair at the same time. Every Sunday night, it served two-dollar spaghetti dinners, and if I played a set of songs, they would give me my dinner for free. I was playing for supper.

Among other things, Hobart helped me raise funds to record a demo recording in New York City in January 1983. By this point, I'd released two CDs for Folkways and was expecting to turn them into a bigger, broader career that would allow me to stop working odd jobs at record stores, bookstores, restaurants, and health food stores. I must have worked in dozens of these locations throughout the years.

Throughout the early 1980s, I lived with a man named Clyde Joseph Woodward III. I had met him through the Houston music scene. Clyde was another of those poets on motorcycles. He was born into a country club family, but that was not the type of person he desired to be. He was a huge man and was quite protective of me, which meant a lot to me at the time. He wasn't a poet in the traditional sense, but he enjoyed poetry and was an avid reader. He wanted to be a musician, but he never put in the necessary effort. My friend, writer Margaret Moser, who was also a close friend of Clyde, once described him as "a cultural chameleon capable of jaw-dropping magic," and I agree. He exuded a lovely charisma that I found really alluring. He may be the life of the party. He was the type of guy who knew where to locate the tastiest crawfish dives in the smallest communities in Louisiana, as well as the finest white-tablecloth restaurants in New Orleans, all while being an authority on the region's traditional music.

Clyde and I would drive around the area, from Houston and Austin to New Orleans and everywhere in between. It was my first relatively long-lasting relationship. We'd go dancing with Margaret and her friends. In the winter of 1982, we attended the memorial service for Lightnin' Hopkins, one of the greatest blues musicians of all time. A guitar-shaped wreath was hung in his honour, and people waited up around the block to pay their condolences. Another time, we were on the road and had nowhere to stay, so we spent the night at Johnny Winter's apartment. I remember conversing with him about Robert Johnson.

Clyde was a lot of fun to be around, but he had another side to him that I either didn't see clearly enough or didn't want to notice during our relationship. He was an alcoholic, and during our time together, his marijuana addiction progressed to cocaine and other amphetamines. He was in a death cycle, combining alcohol's depressive effects with amphetamines. Some of my pals eventually informed me that he was also trafficking narcotics, although he kept this primarily secret from me. Clyde loved and worshipped me, and despite his imperfections, I felt his warmth even when he fucked himself—and us.

When I was researching for this book, I asked David, Brian, and Hobart about this time, and they all remembered Clyde having a negative, distracting impact on those sessions. He was attempting to defend me and serve as my de facto manager, but they saw him as a clumsy bully. Brian even admitted that he was terrified of Clyde. I was completely unaware of this scenario. Brian also stated that Clyde was clearly using cocaine, which caused his mood swings. I didn't notice that until later.

I knew I had to stop my relationship with Clyde when the phone rang when we were at a motel. I grabbed it up, and before I could say anything, the man on the other end hissed, "Where is my money? "Where is my fucking money?" It turned out that the guy had given Clyde a lot of marijuana to sell and was searching for his money. I thought, "Fuck, they're going to come for us. "We are outlaws.

Musically, I was far ahead of where others thought I was. I had a vision, and all I had to do was wait for an opportunity to realise it. The problem for me was that I didn't always know how to explain my vision or articulate it. I was thinking about musicians like Lou Reed and the Velvet Underground, as well as Dylan when he went electric. I wanted to rock long before I was able to. By default, I played guitar and sang songs, so I was immediately classified. "You're this cute girl singing folk songs and country songs, so you're a singer-songwriter." True, I began with that type of music, which provided a solid foundation for me, but I desired to be a literary rock artist. When I heard Chrissie Hynde and the Pretenders' debut album in 1980, I thought, "That's it. This is it. "This is what I want to do." But I had problems expressing what I felt and heard in my thoughts.

After we finished the New York demos, Clyde and I returned to Texas, and I began to realise that I needed to be somewhere else, not with him. It was painful because I cared deeply for Clyde. He did the best he could. After it became evident that the New York demos were not getting me anywhere, David Hirshland paid me a visit in Austin. He lived in San Francisco and tried to govern me from there. He informed me that I could only go so far if I stayed in Texas. I was already feeling this way, but it was intriguing to hear it from his perspective. I began planning my move to Los Angeles. And I had to break up with Clyde.

Chapter 11

Marty, a radical lefty hippie-biker, ran the funky Rockaway Store. He refused to supply Steve Earle's album Guitar Town because one of the songs referenced a "Japanese guitar." Marty was such a lefty that he refused to stock a record that turned out to be Steve's breakthrough.

I also worked at Pecos Bill's Bar-B-Q stand, and I believe I worked at Barnes & Noble, though it could have been another chain bookstore. I felt comfortable at bookstores and record stores. One unique job I had was selling gourmet sausages at stores. I had a cart that I would set up inside a store and sell these delicious sausages to shoppers. I prepared samples and served them with toothpicks. There were several flavours, including apple and maple. I adored that work. I made $75 for the afternoon, and no one harassed me.

One of the best things about Los Angeles in the 1980s was that the music scene was diverse in terms of genre. I felt liberated from Texas' singer-songwriter and cosmic cowboy scenes. Today, you can see a glimpse of my early days in Los Angeles by looking through old issues of the LA Weekly, where my name appears on the same weekly bill as bands like Jane's Addiction, X, the Long Ryders, and the Blasters at clubs like Raji's, the Troubadour, McCabe's, Club Lingerie, and the Palomino. That would never have occurred in Texas. Nobody in Los Angeles inquired or cared about your genre, least of all the club managers and listeners. The record labels, as usual, were sluggish to accept what was going underground.

Dirty garage music mingled with country music in Los Angeles; as far as I know, that was the only place where the mix occurred. The scene featured equal parts X, the Germs, the Blasters, the Ramones, Los Lobos, and Merle Haggard. L.A. marked the beginning of what became known as "alternative country," a term I truly despise. I know I'm often regarded as a pioneer of alt-country and "Americana," and I accept that as an intended compliment, but I reject those terms because they're simply more genres or categories that people—primarily those at record labels—need and cling to for a variety of reasons, the majority of which are commercial.

The mixed-genre scene in Los Angeles is sometimes referred to as the Paisley Underground, which is another phrase I try to avoid. The Long Ryders were one of the ensembles that best exhibited this combination of styles. They were an excellent country rock punk band. I began opening performances for them in late 1984 or 1985. One night at Raji's, a drunk man in the audience heckled me. Between songs, he'd yell, "You need the Long Ryders, you couldn't do it on your own, you aren't anything without the Long Ryders." The guys in the Long Ryders didn't appreciate it, so a barroom battle broke out, and this heckler wound up hospitalised. An LAPD detective contacted and stated that the man was planning to file charges against the band members unless they let him open a few performances. It turned out he was an unhappy musician.

Even though our marriage did not endure, the time Greg and I spent together was immensely beneficial to me professionally. That's when I composed the songs that would appear on my 1988 self-titled album for Rough Trade Records. Greg claims that I wrote all of my best songs during emotionally and psychologically dark moments in my life, when I was unhappy and stressed, and my obsessive-compulsive disorder was at its peak. I don't remember it that way, but I'm confident his observations are correct. I believe that music was my therapy for dealing with many of the traumas I experienced as a child, beginning when I received my guitar at the age of twelve and possibly continuing today at the age of seventy. In general, however, I do not believe that my periodic depression benefits my songwriting or any other aspect of my life. To be honest, I recognize that my erratic mood swings have caused some issues for others at times, when they expect me to do one thing and I do something else instead. I've struggled with something resembling obsessive-compulsive disorder, which frequently appears when I start to feel melancholy. It's as if OCD is a form of coping. As if there is something I should be doing and I chose to reorganise everything in my closets instead of doing it while others wait for me.

Several things happened in Los Angeles that pushed me onward. One was that David and Hobart did an excellent job of packaging and marketing me to venues. I was a part of a series of shows called "Millions of Williams" in the fall of 1985, which included Victoria Williams and the Williams Brothers, the nephews of the legendary singer Andy Williams. Then, for over a year, I had what was known as a residency at Al's Bar, a fantastic club in an abandoned hotel in downtown LA. I played there every week for months, with David Mansfield on guitar and David Miner on bass. They were both members of T Bone Burnett's Alpha Band. Mansfield, of course, was a member of Dylan's Rolling Thunder Revue and had played on my New York tapes a few years prior. He is currently living in Los Angeles. David, David, and I were an excellent trio without a drummer. I wish we'd recorded.

I appreciate the literary connection to a writer I knew from my father's gatherings in Fayetteville. Al's Bar kind of summed up what I was attempting to accomplish. LA Weekly was also incredibly supportive of me, frequently highlighting my shows. Everyone was paying attention to what I was doing.

Raji's was another crucial spot for me. It was a unique location in Hollywood. LA Weekly also described it well: "If you merged the Ramones with the Arabian Nights, you may end up with something similar to this club. His satanic majesty Dobbs provides cold beer and wine, hot Mexican food, and constant rock & roll.

A couple executives from Rounder Records in New York went to Los Angeles to see me perform at Raji's. I didn't have my own band yet, so members of the Long Ryders filled in for me. Everyone was drinking and having a great time. I thought everything was going nicely. But the next day, I met with the executives, who told me, "We like you, but we don't think you're ready to take a band on the road." "Your show is not polished enough." Something similar occurred with Rhino Records, Hightone Records, and others.

I recall driving back to Silver Lake from Beverly Hills and thinking, "Wow, this is fucking incredible. Somebody is giving me a real chance. I was over the moon.

The Columbia agreement gave me plenty of time to finish songs I'd started composing years ago and write new ones. I was able to stop my odd jobs and focus on my music. I'd wake up in my Silver Lake duplex, sit on the back balcony in the morning sun, and write. Then, in the afternoon, while the light shone through the west-facing windows, I'd sit in the living room and create songs. And then Gurf, John, Donald, and I would perform those tunes at nighttime shows.

I composed "Changed the Locks" during my time in Silver Lake. It's a traditional blues song with lyrics about unrequited love, a theme I was familiar with. Those are the easiest songs to create, especially when you are young and experiencing upheaval in many relationships. Same with "Abandoned," which I penned at Silver Lake. Neither of those songs are about somebody in particular, but rather the termination of relationships in general.

One of my favourite songs from my career, "Side of the Road," was written there. I had a tendency to lose myself in relationships, which I was always reflecting on. Many women will surrender to males and lose any sense of themselves. I did that repeatedly. I felt like a bird in a cage that needed to get free. This is how I felt about my marriage to Greg, even though I knew it was equally my fault as his. I'd been in treatment to attempt to keep from losing myself in these men. I was also inspired by an Andrew Wyeth artwork that I saw in a book a few years ago. It was a photo of a lonely woman.

"Passionate Kisses" is about Greg. The Long Ryders were taking off, and he was constantly travelling throughout the United States and Europe. This was the first time I was with someone who was constantly gone. Usually, I was the one that was constantly out or gone. Musically, the song is heavily influenced by Joan Armatrading. "Am I Too Blue" and "Big Red Sun Blues" are both about Greg. Even though our relationship was structurally difficult since we were both full-time artists attempting to advance our professions, I tended to blame the troubles on my personal despair or blues.

I started writing "I Just Wanted to See You So Bad" in 1979 or 1980, but didn't finish it until I had the Columbia deal. It's about Bruce Weigl, a poet who I had a huge crush on. I was living in Houston at the time, and I had a performance in Little Rock while Bruce was giving a poetry reading there. I don't remember how we met. Perhaps he knew my father through the poetry world. In any case, I was instantly smitten. I attended his reading, then he came to my concert. He possessed the rugged, good-looking poet character I indicated, similar to Sam Shepard—handsome, humorous, intelligent, and rough and tumble. The sensitive, masculine guy. Part of me wants to remain up all night discussing philosophy and art, while another part of me wants to be pulled into the bedroom. Bruce was another of these individuals who could do both.

Of course, things did not end well. When I arrived, Bruce decided it was a good moment to inform me that he was married and his wife was expecting. So much for it. But my feelings for Bruce, as well as the anticipation of our meeting in San Antonio, inspired me to write a song that would launch an album that altered my life.

"The Night's Too Long" was completed prior to the Columbia deal. I wrote it shortly after moving to Los Angeles. I want to think of that song as inspired by the film Looking for Mr. Goodbar, but it was also about going out at night and seeing the same women over and over. I went out a lot back then. I was young and unmarried, and as a musician, that is what you do: you go check out other musicians. Certain people appear to be associated with a variety of bands. Perhaps I was one of them. So there was a little of me in that song as well. As a writer, you must have empathy for the individuals you write about. Sylvia was a young woman fleeing to start a new life. That's similar to what I've done before. Sylvia left a small town to move to a big metropolis because she was bored and weary of the small-town folks, and she wanted to meet a guy in a leather jacket. That could have been me going from Austin to Los Angeles, or Greg the guy in the leather jacket.

These were the tracks I planned to record for the demo. They were also the tunes I was performing in live gigs at the time. Columbia hired Henry Lewy to produce my demo. He was a huge deal. He produced all of Joni Mitchell's breakout albums, including Blue, as well as albums by Neil Young and Leonard Cohen. Henry enlisted a lot of prominent artists to perform on my demo, including Garth Hudson from the Band, Terry Adams from NRBQ, and the great New Orleans pianist Henry Butler. I was thrilled and eager to have these famous musicians play my song, but in retrospect, we definitely should have recorded the demo with my usual band rather than this all-star lineup. Ron Oberman and his colleagues at Columbia's Los Angeles offices listened to the resulting demo and declined to offer me a formal record deal. They claimed it was too country for rock. They forwarded the tape to Columbia execs in Nashville, who deemed it too rock for country.

Even though I was terribly disappointed, I was able to muster the energy, with the aid and affirmation of David and Hobart, to go through another round of meetings and showcases with labels, this time with the updated demo. Every one of them abandoned me. We tried huge labels and little labels, and they all passed on me, most of them for the second time.We had met at my place in Silver Lake. After he departed, I pulled out my Neil Young and Bob Dylan LPs to tell myself that it was fine if my songs lacked bridges.

More than three decades later, "Changed the Locks" is still one of my most popular songs, with the same structure as before. Tom Petty, one of my favourite songwriters and musicians, performed an excellent cover of it in 1996. Now it is something to be proud of.

Chapter 12

One thing I've learnt over the years is that putting in hard work will result in some sort of reward. It could be an indirect reward, and it may not come as quickly as you would like, but your enthusiasm and determination will always be appreciated.

I didn't realise this in 1986, thus I was depressed when every label rejected me despite having recorded a significant demo. I pondered relocating back to Texas. To be honest, one of the reasons I hadn't moved back sooner was that so many of my friends in Texas had mocked my first decision to relocate to Los Angeles. Texas has a certain provincial sense to it, as if you have everything you need right there and have no reason to leave. It reminds me of how some New Yorkers feel about New York City. Not all Texans or New Yorkers, but many of them. When I told a few individuals in Texas that I was relocating to Los Angeles, they said, "We'll see you back here in six months or a year." That still bothers me.

The reality was that I was now thirty-three years old, which was considered old for a relatively unknown female singer. It might yet be ancient. I'd spent two years in Los Angeles doing every gig at any place that would take me, and for the majority of that time, I was simultaneously working at energy-sucking day jobs to pay the bills, and now I was back at them. I was fatigued and dejected, but I persevered. I still believed. Gurf, Donald, John, and I continued to perform shows using the repertoire I had devised. They, too, continued to believe.

Around that time, I recorded a song for the compilation album A Town South of Bakersfield. During the session, I collaborated with engineer Dusty Wakeman, who became a lifetime friend. Dusty introduced me to Pete Anderson, who was a well-known musician in Los Angeles at the time, having collaborated and produced Dwight Yoakam. Pete appreciated my music and wanted to help me get a record deal. He formed a band, and I made another demo with him, this time with only four songs on it. I wasn't satisfied with the end result. I called Pete and said, "I don't like this." I told him it was overproduced and did not represent what I intended at all. He responded with something like, "That doesn't really matter. We only need to get our foot in the door, and then we can do whatever we want. I replied that my senses told me that wasn't going to happen, and that even if it did, I wouldn't be satisfied with the outcome. I had an intrinsic fear of being overproduced and too polished. None of the albums I admired were overproduced and polished. I was anxious that record executives would hear this new tape and assume it was the type of record I wanted to make.

One day, when things seemed dire and I was sitting around the Silver Lake apartment, Greg was on the road with the Long Ryders, and nothing was happening in my career except the same shows around Los Angeles, my phone rang. It was a man named Robin Hurley from Rough Trade Records, the British punk label that had recently, unbeknownst to me, opened an office in San Francisco called Rough Trade America. Copies of my Columbia demo tape circulated, and tracks from it were occasionally played on college or independent radio stations. I'm not sure how Robin found out about it, but he got his hands on the Columbia demo. He also discovered my Folkways album Happy Woman Blues, which he thoroughly enjoyed.

One of the advantages of working with a smaller studio budget was that we simply had to go in and do it. No fucking around. When I originally got the deal, Gurf and I discussed which producers to approach, but we didn't have the budget, which turned out to be a blessing. An acquaintance once asked me, "Why don't you and Gurf just produce it yourselves?" The songs were already ready because the band and I had played them so many times at performances. We could go into the studio and play the songs as if we had performed them live. That is probably how the majority of the punk bands on Rough Trade did it. We'll do it, I reasoned. So we did. In June 1988, we recorded the record at Dusty Wakeman's Mad Dog Studios in Venice Beach. We only spent a few weeks, and the record was complete. I believe we did about one song per day. It was a more organic approach, one I still favour now.

My life altered after the record was released in 1988. I was prepared for it. I was thirty-five years old and had been performing music almost every day since I was twelve, doing day jobs to make things meet. Rough Trade took me to Europe and around the US. It was the first time I was able to tell myself, "Wow, I am doing this." I make a living by playing music and singing. "It is working." I've been able to do this ever since.

Sometimes I remember back to that small duplex apartment in Silver Lake where the majority of the Rough Trade songs were created, when I had no idea how things would turn out. I remember leaving the flat in the dark and going for a walk on Silver Lake one night, or perhaps early in the morning before the light came up. I went through the neighbourhood until I arrived at a vista overlooking a baseball field, where the lights were on despite the fact that there was no game or anything going on. There were no individuals present, but the field was lit up. There was a small group of coyotes roaming the ball field. I stood there, watching them from a distance. The field must have been watered on a regular basis to keep the grass alive, therefore I'm presuming the coyotes would visit and suck water off the grass. I just stood there, watching.

Chapter 13

The success of the Rough Trade album introduced new kinds of demands that I had never experienced before. The pressure was now less about how to make a living and more about what I was going to do next. Everyone would ask me, "What are you working on now?" I didn't appreciate the sense of having to meet a standard that I had established for myself. I knew I needed to write new songs that were as good as the ones on that LP. But I had my whole life to write those tunes. Some of those tunes had been boiling in my mind for years before I began performing them or writing them down.

All of the major labels that had previously turned me down were now contacting me and attempting to sign me. They wanted me now, but I didn't want to sign with a major label. Fuck those big labels. I wanted to stay at Rough Trade because they were so supportive of me when no one else was, and it seemed like a small family. However, I was quickly discovering that they had limited resources. Record stores would only order a set amount of Rough Trade albums. They lacked the promotional and distribution reach of a larger label.

Then I received an offer from Bob Buziak at RCA. The only reason I considered it was Bob's cool personality and decent reputation. He had signed many excellent, edgy musicians, like the Cowboy Junkies and Treat Her Right, whose lead vocalist went on to form the band Morphine. I was dumb and naive enough to believe that Rough Trade and RCA could collaborate, resulting in Rough Trade/RCA. I decided to sign with RCA, which was a harsh decision that I later regretted. Rough Trade attempted to sue me for breach of contract, but my lawyer learned they had allowed the recording agreement to expire, and I was free to leave. I remained friendly with Robin Hurley, and when we released the twenty-fifth anniversary edition of that album, I asked him to write an essay for the liner notes, which he did beautifully.

Almost as soon as I signed with RCA, Bob Buziak left to work at Elektra Records. I didn't blame Bob for leaving, and I eventually realised why he left: he was trapped in a stifling corporate bureaucracy. So here I was, contractually bound to RCA without the main reason I had considered joining with them in the first place—

Bob. The new person who came in to replace Bob had recently transferred from Nashville. I can't remember his name, but everyone said he was "a numbers man."

RCA wanted "Six Blocks Away" to be the first single, so we began working on it first. We completed an initial mix of the song, which was then delivered to RCA's New York office for Dave Thoener to remix for radio. I'd never dealt with a process like this before. This was before digital recording, so they transmitted the rough mix to New York on a hard-copy tape by FedEx, UPS, or whatever. It felt as if something really valuable was being let go and taken to an unknown location where others might mess with it. This felt even worse than the guys gazing over our shoulders.

One day, Kaufman contacted me from his Beverly Hills office and said, "Hey, I received the remixed track back from New York. Come to my office, and we'll listen to it. So I headed over to Beverly Hills, and by this point, I had a serious attitude problem. I stepped into Kaufman's office, and he played the song. He hopped up and down in his Gucci shoes, saying, "Isn't this great? It sounds like a record now. It sounds like a real record," as if it hadn't sounded like one before Thoener got his slick paws on it. He had pushed the bass and drums to the front and my vocals to the back, as was common in early 1990s pop mixing. To be fair, Thoener likely did this because he was hired to do it that way.

"I fucking hate this," I admitted. "I hate it." Even though I advised them, they sought to release this remix as a single. I fought them every step of the way. I was correct. It sounded terrible.

During this time, I was invited to South by Southwest in Austin to participate in a public panel discussion titled "How Does Commercialism Affect Creativity?". Oh, man. It was perfect. Now I had a platform to share my tale.

When it was my turn to speak in Austin, I laid everything out just as it had at RCA. I was very honest. The next day, I received a call from my irate manager. He worked for one of the most prominent promoters in the industry. He responded: "Congratulations, you got kicked off RCA." He was unhappy about it, but I was overjoyed. I was free. I ended up signing with Bob Buziak again, this time at

Chameleon, a subsidiary of Elektra Records where he was now employed.

One of the songs I created during this time, "Little Angel, Little Brother," is still one of my favourites, and possibly the best song I've ever written. It's a sombre tribute to my brother, Robert, who is two years younger than me. It's a collection of photographs and impressions I had of my wonderful younger brother, with a hint of sadness. He read all of Shakespeare and memorised a lot of it. He had the potential to become a great musician. He was incredibly talented. After high school, he spent much of his time in New Orleans, where my mother lived, and he once performed as a one-man musical show under the stage name Rockin' Bob. He played the piano and sang quite well. However, there would be extended intervals when I had no idea where he was. When I was still married to Greg, the Long Ryders performed in New Orleans, and Greg spent some time looking for Robert but was unsuccessful. He occasionally visited my mother's residence. He would show up and play her piano for hours on end, staying for days, weeks, or even months at a time. Then he would disappear for a bit before reappearing. Something had occurred to him, which I still don't comprehend today. I can only speak to my own childhood traumas and hardships; I have no idea what Robert's were.

Chameleon released Sweet Old World in 1992. One of the songs that stands out is "Hot Blood" because it was the first time I wrote directly about lust, which is something that women aren't meant to do, despite the fact that males have sung songs about lust throughout rock and roll history. To mention a few, examples include "Brown Sugar" and "Let's Spend the Night Together" by the Stones, "The Lemon Song" by Zeppelin, "Foxey Lady" by Hendrix, "Light My Fire" by the Doors, "Sexual Healing" by Marvin Gaye, and nearly everything James Brown ever performed.

"Hot Blood" was not based on anyone in particular. I envisioned a female character for the point of view in that song, yet, like all of the characters, I imagine a little of myself in there.

By this time, I had moved to Nashville. Steve Earle, Emmylou Harris, and Rosanne Cash were living there at the time. John Prine was present. Nanci Griffiths. By that point, I knew several of these musicians personally. It seemed like a decent location for me to be. Greg and I had already split up, so it was time to move on.

But I didn't have a great mindset when I first arrived in Nashville. I despised what had happened to country music. I struggled with the concept of two, three, four, or even five or six individuals writing a song together. I didn't like the sound of modern country music at the time, or how slickly it was recorded. It didn't help that shortly after I arrived in town, I was invited to appear on the TV show Crook & Chase, an early morning coffee and breakfast show. I agreed. It would be good exposure, I reasoned. When I told the producers I wanted to play my song "Pineola," they reacted negatively. They said it was too dark. It wasn't "good morning music," they claimed. It did not meet their definition of wholesome American morning music. However, it was the only song I wanted to perform on their show, so I stuck to my guns. They finally succumbed, but it left a nasty taste in my mouth. It pressed my rebel buttons. I had a feeling Nashville wouldn't work for me.

Later that year, something very good happened. Mary Chapin Carpenter recorded "Passionate Kisses" and it rose to the top of the charts, introducing my work to a whole new audience of popular music enthusiasts. I received a Grammy for Best Country tune for the tune. My reaction was mixed. Of course, I was flattered and pleased, and I was grateful to Carpenter for giving me this opportunity, but I was also timid and afraid. The prospect of really attending the Grammy ceremony, for example, was extremely daunting. My thoughts were racing: "What am I going to wear? Will I look good? "Are my teeth pretty enough?" I was staring at myself via a microscope.

The truth is that I was both self-conscious and afraid. I was afraid that I didn't belong. It's a sensation I've been attempting to overcome my entire life. It's a puzzle that I feel many artists have attempted to solve for centuries. It takes immense bravery to produce the work in the first place, but when it comes time to share it with the world, the confidence required to do so is unrelated to the daring that generated the piece. I'm not as afraid as I once was, but it still creeps up on me now and then.

Chapter 14

Sweet Old World provided me additional attention and chances, including invitations to perform at events and festivals all over the world, as well as offers to sing on other people's records. I spent the majority of the next two years on the road. I loved—and continue to love—being on the road, living in buses and motels. I still follow that pattern at home today.

During that Sweet Old World tour, I became acquainted with Roly Salley, who was a member of my band. He was a veteran bass player in Chris Isaak's band and has also performed with John Prine. He was a bassist in my band during the Sweet Old World tour. He was another of the hilarious, bright, and enigmatic men who came into my life and inspired numerous songs on my next album, Car Wheels on a Gravel Road.

Roly chased me relentlessly, and I was instantly captivated with him. We had an uncommon sexual chemistry and became highly entangled with one another. The songs "Joy" and "Still I Long For Your Kiss" are about Roly. Gurf had pulled me aside at a bar one night and warned me about Roly. But I completely fell down the rabbit hole. I took my relationship with Roly extremely seriously, and I remember thinking, "We're going to buy a house together." When I start thinking about buying a house, you know I need to be careful.

I was still in a committed relationship with another man, Lorne, when Roly began chasing me. We were in New York City one night when Lorne arrived for the concerts. So we were all in the same hotel. I thought I needed to be mature about the matter and inform Lorne about my feelings for Roly. Lorne didn't say anything. He began taking up items from the hotel room—lamps, chairs, tables, and the television—and throwing them as hard as he could against the wall. I was afraid as I sat on the side of the bed. I was terrified he'd hurt me, but he didn't.

I finally got out of the hotel room and into the lobby, where I summoned my tour manager, who rushed up to Lorne's room to calm him down. After a while, my tour manager informed me that I might return to my accommodation. Lorne had bought a six-pack of

Budweiser and was sitting on the bed, drinking it. He alternated between crying and yelling at me. We remained up all night talking about how this was the end of our relationship.

The next morning, I bid farewell to Lorne, bless his heart, and climbed up the steps to the tour bus, where I sat next to Roly. You can see what's coming now, but I couldn't then. "I broke up with Lorne, so I'm free now," I told Roly. "I'm yours." He immediately had an expression on his face that I had never seen before, as if he was stunned and terrified, thinking, "Oh my God, what the fuck?" Everything between us shifted in that instant. At one point, he stated, "We have to get off this metal firecracker," referring to the tour bus, "because everything is going to explode." He meant, let's wait until we finish the tour before we continue. Of course, that never occurred. When we got off the metal firecracker, our relationship went to shit. He did not fulfil his pledge. But he kept me hooked for a time.

I was at a strawberry festival in Northern California shortly after the tour ended, and I was still quite interested in him. The event organisers had placed me up in one of these log cabins with no phones. There was a phone booth located in the parking lot. I went into the phone booth and called Roly, saying, "I am sick and tired of this bullshit. "I need to know where I stand.

"I love you but this relationship doesn't fit into my agenda right now," he told you.

"Okay," I replied and hung up. I went into my room and screamed and cried. I later discovered that he was associated with several women at the same time he was with me, some of them were prominent musicians. I will not name names. That relationship ended, but I got a good song out of it, which would appear on my Car Wheels album.

Chapter 15

The success of the Rough Trade album introduced new kinds of demands that I had never experienced before. The pressure was now less about how to make a living and more about what I was going to do next. Everyone would ask me, "What are you working on now?" I didn't appreciate the sense of having to meet a standard that I had established for myself. I knew I needed to write new songs that were as good as the ones on that LP. But I had my whole life to write those tunes. Some of those tunes had been boiling in my mind for years before I began performing them or writing them down.

All of the major labels that had previously turned me down were now contacting me and attempting to sign me. They wanted me now, but I didn't want to sign with a major label. Fuck those big labels. I wanted to stay at Rough Trade because they were so supportive of me when no one else was, and it seemed like a small family. However, I was quickly discovering that they had limited resources. Record stores would only order a set amount of Rough Trade albums. They lacked the promotional and distribution reach of a larger label.

Then I received an offer from Bob Buziak at RCA. The only reason I considered it was Bob's cool personality and decent reputation. He had signed many excellent, edgy musicians, like the Cowboy Junkies and Treat Her Right, whose lead vocalist went on to form the band Morphine. I was dumb and naive enough to believe that Rough Trade and RCA could collaborate, resulting in Rough Trade/RCA. I decided to sign with RCA, which was a harsh decision that I later regretted. Rough Trade attempted to sue me for breach of contract, but my lawyer learned they had allowed the recording agreement to expire, and I was free to leave. I remained friendly with Robin Hurley, and when we released the twenty-fifth anniversary edition of that album, I asked him to write an essay for the liner notes, which he did beautifully.

Almost as soon as I signed with RCA, Bob Buziak left to work at Elektra Records. I didn't blame Bob for leaving, and I eventually realised why he left: he was trapped in a stifling corporate bureaucracy. So here I was, contractually bound to RCA without the main reason I had considered joining with them in the first place—

Bob. The new person who came in to replace Bob had recently transferred from Nashville. I can't remember his name, but everyone said he was "a numbers man."

RCA wanted "Six Blocks Away" to be the first single, so we began working on it first. We completed an initial mix of the song, which was then delivered to RCA's New York office for Dave Thoener to remix for radio. I'd never dealt with a process like this before. This was before digital recording, so they transmitted the rough mix to New York on a hard-copy tape by FedEx, UPS, or whatever. It felt as if something really valuable was being let go and taken to an unknown location where others might mess with it. This felt even worse than the guys gazing over our shoulders.

When it was my turn to speak in Austin, I laid everything out just as it had at RCA. I was very honest. The next day, I received a call from my irate manager. He worked for one of the most prominent promoters in the industry. He responded: "Congratulations, you got kicked off RCA." He was unhappy about it, but I was overjoyed. I was free. I ended up signing with Bob Buziak again, this time at Chameleon, a subsidiary of Elektra Records where he was now employed.

One of the songs I created during this time, "Little Angel, Little Brother," is still one of my favourites, and possibly the best song I've ever written. It's a sombre tribute to my brother, Robert, who is two years younger than me. It's a collection of photographs and impressions I had of my wonderful younger brother, with a hint of sadness. He read all of Shakespeare and memorised a lot of it. He had the potential to become a great musician. He was incredibly talented. After high school, he spent much of his time in New Orleans, where my mother lived, and he once performed as a one-man musical show under the stage name Rockin' Bob. He played the piano and sang quite well. However, there would be extended intervals when I had no idea where he was. When I was still married to Greg, the Long Ryders performed in New Orleans, and Greg spent some time looking for Robert but was unsuccessful. He occasionally visited my mother's residence. He would show up and play her piano for hours on end, staying for days, weeks, or even months at a time. Then he would disappear for a bit before reappearing. Something had occurred to him, which I still don't comprehend today. I can only speak to my own childhood traumas and hardships; I have no idea what Robert's were.

Chameleon released Sweet Old World in 1992. One of the songs that stands out is "Hot Blood" because it was the first time I wrote directly about lust, which is something that women aren't meant to do, despite the fact that males have sung songs about lust throughout rock and roll history. To mention a few, examples include "Brown Sugar" and "Let's Spend the Night Together" by the Stones, "The Lemon Song" by Zeppelin, "Foxey Lady" by Hendrix, "Light My Fire" by the Doors, "Sexual Healing" by Marvin Gaye, and nearly everything James Brown ever performed.

"Hot Blood" was not based on anyone in particular. I envisioned a female character for the point of view in that song, yet, like all of the characters, I imagine a little of myself in there.

By this time, I had moved to Nashville. Steve Earle, Emmylou Harris, and Rosanne Cash were living there at the time. John Prine was present. Nanci Griffiths. By that point, I knew several of these musicians personally. It seemed like a decent location for me to be. Greg and I had already split up, so it was time to move on.

But I didn't have a great mindset when I first arrived in Nashville. I despised what had happened to country music. I struggled with the concept of two, three, four, or even five or six individuals writing a song together. I didn't like the sound of modern country music at the time, or how slickly it was recorded. It didn't help that shortly after I arrived in town, I was invited to appear on the TV show Crook & Chase, an early morning coffee and breakfast show. I agreed. It would be good exposure, I reasoned. When I told the producers I wanted to play my song "Pineola," they reacted negatively. They said it was too dark. It wasn't "good morning music," they claimed. It did not meet their definition of wholesome American morning music. However, it was the only song I wanted to perform on their show, so I stuck to my guns. They finally succumbed, but it left a nasty taste in my mouth. It pressed my rebel buttons. I had a feeling Nashville wouldn't work for me.

Later that year, something very good happened. Mary Chapin Carpenter recorded "Passionate Kisses" and it rose to the top of the charts, introducing my work to a whole new audience of popular music enthusiasts. I received a Grammy for Best Country tune for the tune. My reaction was mixed. Of course, I was flattered and pleased, and I was grateful to Carpenter for giving me this opportunity, but I was also timid and afraid. The prospect of really attending the Grammy ceremony, for example, was extremely daunting. My thoughts were racing: "What am I going to wear? Will I look good? "Are my teeth pretty enough?" I was staring at myself via a microscope.

The truth is that I was both self-conscious and afraid. I was afraid that I didn't belong. It's a sensation I've been attempting to overcome my entire life. It's a puzzle that I feel many artists have attempted to solve for centuries. It takes immense bravery to produce the work in the first place, but when it comes time to share it with the world, the confidence required to do so is unrelated to the daring that generated the piece. I'm not as afraid as I once was, but it still creeps up on me now and then.

Chapter 16

I signed with Rick Rubin's label, but Gurf was to co-produce the new record with me rather than Rick. Gurf's demands began to feel like a barrier to my progress. If he truly desired complete control over his music, I believed he should go out on his own. At one point, Rick approached me and asked, "Have you ever considered working with other musicians? Forming a new band?" At first, the concept terrified me. "Oh, no," I told him. "This is my band." "I am loyal to them." I was protective of those guys. They had stuck with me while I was establishing my profession in Los Angeles.

But, truthfully, I was already feeling constrained. I wanted to avoid the conflict. Rick recognized that while this specific band had had a successful run, if I wanted to explore new artistic areas, I might have to form a new one.

Despite these reservations, we began recording the new album later in 1995, with the same band and Gurf on producing duties. We started working at Arlyn Studios in Austin, which was partially owned by Willie Nelson. Rick was unable to join us in the studio, so we would ship recordings overnight to him in Los Angeles and wait for his feedback on the tunes.

During this period, I was having these dumb flirtations with different men. I remember this young writer who was maybe fifteen or twenty years younger than myself. We were standing in front of my house in Nashville one night, enjoying the crisp fall air. I was attempting to emulate what I had seen my father do: invite friends around to share a meal. Thanksgiving fueled my drive to host, to emulate my father. Now I was with a younger writer whom I had recently met. I wanted him to be clever and witty, and I wanted to fall in love. But he wasn't very clever or humorous, and I wasn't in love. Nonetheless, I was determined to transform him into the ideal I imagined. So we kissed repeatedly. I imagined I could transform him into a poet prince, someone my father would approve of, someone who would take me with him on his voyage through clouds of poetry, universities, and workshops. I was always looking for the next amazing poet. That's what I wanted—or thought I wanted. So I hung on. We kissed repeatedly. I'd owe him an apology letter. He wouldn't owe me anything. We'd meet again to share blushing moments and memories. Nothing more. Nothing less.

During this time, Steve Earle requested me to sing on his song "You're Still Standing There" from his album I Feel Alright, which was released the following year. I visited Ray Kennedy's studio to record my vocals. Steve had collaborated with Ray on almost everything he had ever done. Ray's studio was stocked with vintage guitars and other vintage equipment that he had accumulated over the years. I would describe him as having a vintage manner of doing things, despite the fact that he is well-versed in modern technologies. I really liked how my vocals sounded in Ray's production of Steve's tune. Steve sent me a copy of his album's rough mixes, and I fell in love with the sound Ray was getting. Bells rang in my head: this is how I want my record to sound.

That's how it began. We were merely going to recut "Jackson," and everyone agreed except Gurf. The recuts sounded so good that we decided to recut the entire record.

Unfortunately, the hostility between Gulf and I simply grew. Something needed to give. It was unsustainable. We decided to have another break. Gurf never returned, and I never invited him back.

Making records can mean many different things. It could be exciting. It can get tedious. It can be stressful. And it can be exhausting. It has the potential to push everyone engaged to their limits. That is now something I accept as normal.

Even with Gurf out of the picture, there was still pressure to complete the record, and anxiety rose. I am very deliberate, and I dislike being rushed; if I need to redo a voice, I simply want to be able to do it. No questions were asked.

One day, I stepped into Ray's studio and told Steve and Ray, "I want to redo my vocal on 'Lake Charles.'" Steve replied, "No, you don't have to do that. When will you trust someone, Lu?"

But I persisted, and Steve finally said, "Lu, it's just a record for God's sakes, come on, get over it."

"It's not just a record," I explained. He thought I was underestimating myself, that he knew better, and, to be fair, he thought I was smart and told me so, but he also said I was driving him insane. One night, I burst into sobs and lay in the foetal position in my voice booth. I had difficulties feeling overwhelmed by pressure on occasion, and one of my fight-or-flight responses was to simply check out in whatever way I could.

A few days later, Steve arrived at the studio and announced, "I'm finished. That is it. I'm fucking buying a ticket to New Orleans and getting out of here. "I have had it." He did not actually leave, but he had made his point. He stayed until we finished everything and then left to continue on the road.

However, I believed there were a few more details on the record that needed to be included.

My bass player, John, was pals with Roy Bittan, a longstanding keyboardist in the E Street Band, and suggested we contact Roy for the finishing touches. Roy was doing his own engineering and production work in Los Angeles while he wasn't on tour with Springsteen, and he told John he'd be delighted to collaborate with us. We flew down to Los Angeles and worked with Roy at Rumbo Studios in Canoga Park.

We ultimately finished the album, despite all of the turmoil with Gurf, the tension between me and Steve, the several studios and towns, and the mounting recording expenditures. I believed we'd reached the finish line. Then, unbelievably, a large new impediment surfaced. Rick Rubin's label, American, was in the process of moving distribution companies, so he opted to hold Car Wheels until the new distribution agreement was finalised.

Rick delayed releasing the record for two years.

It had been five years since Sweet Old World, and I still hadn't released a new record. Rumours circulated about how difficult I was to work with. There was a big, horrible feature story about me in The New York Times Magazine that unfairly fueled the suspicions. The writer portrayed me as a control freak. The title of his essay was "Lucinda Williams Is in Pain." To my knowledge, the writer had never written about the recording process, and he had no idea how messy it can be. Yes, this process was especially difficult, and I am well aware that there are instances when I can add an extra layer of unforeseen emotion to an already difficult circumstance. I had a vision that I was determined to carry out perfectly. It's not always simple to explain that kind of vision, and if musicians you've known for years can't comprehend you, no stranger can either. When Emmylou Harris heard this story, she gave me some valuable advice: never invite a writer into your recording studio. I learned the lesson the hard way.

Throughout this time, I performed in as many shows as possible to earn money and have fun. Many individuals, including musicians and members of my team, contacted Rick to inquire about my record. People were furious with him because they believed he was causing significant damage to my career by holding the album. However, Rick was unconvinced. Finally, my manager, Frank Callari, who had known Rick from their early days in New York, decided to try a fresh approach. He was aware of Rick's spiritual side, and Frank shared that interest. Frank contacted Rick one night at home and told him, "Dude, you have to do this, guy. It is a spiritual thing. Look into your third eye, Rick, and tell me you don't see why Lu's record needs to be released.

"I see," Rick replied, and he agreed to release the record.

But my record still hadn't found a home. There was another unexpected hiccup in the process.

Rosemary Carroll, my attorney for almost my whole career and still today, gave a copy of the song to her husband, Danny Goldberg, the head of Mercury Records, and Danny loved it. He enjoyed it so much that he pushed Mercury's upper management to issue a check for $450,000 to purchase my contract from Rick at American. I didn't know the specifics of this transaction until many years later. All I knew was that there was a good label eager to release the record sooner than Rick had anticipated.

When the record went into production at Mercury, we had to make judgments on the packaging and cover art, which was another source of stress. The Mercury Public Relations staff were hesitant about using Shelby Lee Adams' images, but eventually agreed. Adams was from eastern Kentucky, although he lived in Boston and taught at one of its institutions. He came down to Nashville with one aide to help him move stuff. Mercury dispatched numerous public relations representatives down from New York for the shoot.

I didn't want the public relations images in the album; I wanted Shelby Adams and Birney Imes' photos. I was having trouble deciding which of their photographs to use, and I knew I'd have to work hard with the PR team to acquire what I wanted. I was sitting in my kitchen in Nashville when my attorney, Rosemary, called and told me, "Lucinda, I don't care if this record comes out in a brown paper bag. You must decide now which artwork you want on the record. This is the end of the story. I used the Imes photo for the cover and the Adams photo for the rear cover. Mercury luckily agreed with my decisions.

Car Wheels was eventually available in 1998, six years after Sweet Old World. It earned a Grammy for Best Contemporary Folk Album and remains my best-selling album today.

My relationship with Gurf has been a difficult element of the aftermath of the Car Wheels saga, which continues to this day. It happened 25 years ago, and he still won't speak to me today. I don't know why, and he won't tell anyone, including mutual friends. He continues to believe that his Car Wheels mixes are superior to those released, and he expresses this openly.

I have extended an olive branch to Gurf countless times. Tom and I went to see Gurf perform at a little bar in Los Angeles a few years ago. This was not long after our old band's bassist, John Ciambotti, went away. Our drummer, Donald Lindley, had died a decade ago, leaving Gurf and me as the band's only remaining members. Both deaths occurred suddenly. I figured it was finally time to make things right with Gurf. Also, Tom had never met him. I was hoping we would be able to clear the air. I made an effort to attend his event, and I hoped it meant something to him. Instead, he dusted us off. The next day, he sent me an email that read, "Please stay out of my life." Tom was enraged, and when you mention Gurf to him today, he still gets riled up. It has torn my heart for a long time, but I can finally accept that we will never be able to mend fences, even if I still wonder, "How can someone be that bitter after all these years?"

Chapter 17

When Car Wheels was being prepped for release, Danny Goldberg had the idea to have filmmaker Paul Schrader create a video or short film based on "Right in Time." I typically refused to produce videos for any of my songs, but Schrader had worked on several famous films and written scripts with Martin Scorsese for films such as Raging Bull and Taxi Driver. He also directed his own film, Mishima, which had some good music produced by Philip Glass and performed by the classical string ensemble the Kronos Quartet. I am no film expert, but I agreed that this sounded like a topic worth discussing. Schrader flew down to Nashville to meet with me and address the situation.

The expression "sex, drugs, and rock and roll" implies that the only individuals who get out of hand and behave in dubious ways are rock and roll performers. However, in my perspective, musicians live a cleaner lifestyle than the aforementioned literary figures and those I later encountered in Hollywood. I've spent a lot of time with male musicians over the years, and the majority of them keep things professional.

When Richard returned to our table from the restroom, I should have stood up and left. But we stayed and had dinner. We then visited Skull's, a bar in Nashville's Printer's Alley neighbourhood. For a long period, it was the town's famed tavern. When we were at Skull's, I went to the bathroom, and Schrader turned to Richard and said, "When you get home later tonight and Lucinda is in bed, tell her you think my video ideas are good. Try convincing her with some nice pillow talk." Richard told me that later, and I laughed. Does this guy think I'll be a pushover like that? People in the music business had realised that trying to screw with me would never succeed.

Schrader intended to set the video in a 1940s antiques business run by a husband and wife, with me as the wife. The husband would then be called to battle in Europe, leaving the woman alone. The night before he left, the couple was seen dancing about the antiques shop.

My career took off when Car Wheels was released. I signed a contract for a new six-album deal with Lost Highway, a division of Mercury led by Luke Lewis, who was always a pleasure to work with, very smart and sincere. Basically, I had to create an album every year for six years. The entire framework of my existence shifted. I had more money, two tour buses, and additional duties. I had this consistent thing for the first time in my life. I was in my late forties, and I was prepared for it. Prior to this, my work was inconsistent, and my life was chaotic. Things were now happening consistently, and I could see farther down the road. I do not recall feeling any pressure to create six new albums. It felt thrilling.

Nashville was evolving into a party scene by the end of the 1990s. That's when Ryan Adams arrived in town. It was significant that he relocated to Nashville because young musicians like him typically relocate to Los Angeles or New York. He was about twenty-five years old and had led the major country rock band Whiskeytown. This was before he released any of his own work. At the time, Ryan and I were both managed by Frank Callari.

A year or two after the release of Car Wheels, Frank took me to see Ryan at 12th and Porter, a prominent Nashville restaurant with a small performance room on the other side. Ryan was alone with his guitar and harmonica, dressed in jeans, a T-shirt, and a denim jacket, as he usually is. He began playing, and I stood there utterly amazed. I remember standing next to Frank and seeing this kid—he was a kid, really—sing these great tunes with such presence and projection. He sang some songs that later appeared on his debut solo album, Heartbreaker, which I still believe is fantastic. I turned to Frank and exclaimed, "Oh my God, he's a genius." After that, I was completely smitten and astonished by everything about him. Apparently, he was also impressed with me. He knew about my records.

Ryan and I both adored Frank, so it was only natural that we would spend time together. One night, we were all at a bar, including Frank and Ryan, as well as two girls who worked for Frank. When I wanted to drink, I used to order beer with tequila shots. I preferred wine, but there was no good wine in Nashville bars at the time. Ryan introduced me to vodka tonics, and it was the beginning of the end.

What transpired between Ryan and I is practically meaningless because it was not a genuine love affair. It was simply a flirtation. Ryan enjoyed flirting, and so did I. Flirting is highly undervalued. Ryan was 21 years younger than me, but that didn't matter.

We connected on a variety of musical and intellectual levels, and there was immediate appreciation and understanding. But, given our age gap, the thought of a meaningful relationship was completely out of the question, so nobody considered it. It was impossible. However, that impossibility allows things to happen.

After a few vodka tonics one night, as we were laughing and having fun, Ryan leaned over to me and whispered, "We need to go somewhere and make out." So we proceeded to the patio outside the bar, where we began rolling around and kissing. At some point, I bit his lip. That's just how I am in heated circumstances like that, and many guys appreciate it. Then I bit his lips again. He pulled back and warned, "Don't bite." I said, "Sorry," and he stood up and walked away. I did not hear from him again for several months.

Chapter 18

I recall listening to other musicians when I was younger and thought, "I don't want everything to sound the same. I want to be eclectic and use several styles." I wanted to be someone like Bob Dylan or Neil Young, who could basically do whatever they wanted. Not many women have that opportunity. Everyone wants to keep them in some type of preset box. Bob Dylan and Neil Young can make albums in a variety of styles, but they are always themselves. Even as a child, I aspired to be just that. My husband, Tom, just informed me that he read somewhere that said, "All of Lucinda's records are different, but at the centre, they always retain Lucinda." I consider it as the utmost compliment.

I wanted to go in a different path with my next record. I had won a Grammy for Car Wheels, so I assumed many people would expect a similar follow-up, but I wanted to do something different. Fans become quite attached to the narrative tracks on Car Wheels— "Drunken Angel," "Lake Charles," and "Greenville"—I believe because they identify with the characters. But I wanted to move away from story songs and focus more on the overall sound. I wanted to create an album in which the music took precedence over the lyrics—more about a mood and a groove than a story to tell. But I was stuck: I knew that if I released a record like Car Wheels, some people would say, "This is similar to Car Wheels but not as good." If I built something different, some people would claim it doesn't sound like Car Wheels and hence isn't as good.

I'm not sure what in my makeup prompted me to take this chance and shift my style from something that had finally been very popular to something new, but it was the most significant transition of my career. When I first started working on the song "Are You Down," which has fewer lyrics than my previous songs, I recall thinking, "Wow, I like this, but can I really make records with songs like this?" I had a breakthrough when I discovered I could.

If I'm honest, one thing that may have pushed me in this way was that after Car Wheels came out, everyone began lumping me in with Americana or alt-country, both of which I despise, as I previously stated. They are really restrictive. I understood that people were trying to be complimentary, but it still bothered me, so on some level, I told myself, "I'm going to do something different." That is just my nature.

When I finished writing the songs for Essence, I submitted them to my father, as I always did, because he'd make minor ideas for changing a word here and there, and, who am I kidding, I was also looking for his approval, which I've had to go through in therapy. I was concerned about delivering him these new songs because they were so different and had less words overall. After reading the lyrics, he called me and remarked, "Honey, this is the closest you've come to pure poetry yet."

"Really?" I asked.

"Yeah, you've graduated."

I recall him using the phrase "graduated," and it prompted me to reflect on my career and identify other moments where I had graduated and moved on to bigger, better, and more independent endeavours. I didn't feel compelled to keep sending my music to my father after that.

While I was working on the songs for Essence, Dylan's album Time Out of Mind, produced by Daniel Lanois, came out, and I really like it. It was magnificent lyrically, musically, and sonically. That's the sound and feel I was hoping for on my upcoming album. I was also listening to Sade's album Lovers Rock, released in 2000. It had a feel that was consistent throughout the album's music, which ranged from reggae and dub to rock, folk, soul, and R&B.

I was a nomad in both music and life; about this time, I returned to Los Angeles. Nicholas Hill, a writer and musician friend of mine, had a radio show on a nice station in East Orange, New Jersey, that you could listen to in New York City. I would listen whenever I was in the vicinity. He played a lot of independent artists who played blues, folk, and rock, and he was constantly discovering new talent. He came to Los Angeles shortly after I moved back and brought me Mia Doi Todd's CD. I recall when we were travelling in his rented car and he inserted the CD into the player. I was immediately struck. She is unique. Her music was reminiscent of Suzanne Vega.

Extremely plain and stark. She served as another source of inspiration.

Some people told me I was brave for trying something new, but I was truly terrified at the moment. I wasn't sure if it would work, and I had a major new contract with Lost Highway. The stakes were higher. It would be tremendously embarrassing if my debut record for them was a flop. They signed me based on the success of Car Wheels and the Rough Trade album. This new record would not be like either of those.

I already had "Blue" and "Bus to Baton Rouge," which were old songs, and I thought I'd put them on the record to please the people who wanted the narrative stuff, but I could record them in a different style, and the rest of the record would be all about the groove.

Essence was recorded quite quickly. I demoed the songs with guitarist Bo Ramsey, just the two of us. It was exciting for me in ways other than music since I'd always had a love for him, so being around him was enjoyable. When I sent the sample to Lost Highway, Luke Lewis flipped out. He went on: "This is so good we could release the record just like this." So Bo and I agreed to co-produce the CD. I felt elated.

I did not want to record with my travelling band at the moment. We'd just spent two years on the road, and those guys were fantastic, but I felt like we'd perfected the sound that I was now trying to break away from.

Bo and my manager, Frank Callari, proposed a variety of players, and we ended up with an excellent band for the recordings. We recruited Dylan's bassist, Tony Garnier, and guitarist, Charlie Sexton, as well as the great drummer Jim Keltner, and Bo and Ryan Adams also played guitar. Jim Lauderdale sang harmony vocals on the album, as he did on Car Wheels.

Before we began recording, Bo, Frank, and I went to see Jim Dickinson, the engineer who produced the Replacements' breakout album, Pleased to Meet Me. He lived with his wife in a trailer in Coldwater, Mississippi, near Memphis. They'd purchased a lot of land and put a trailer on it with the aim of building a nice house. But it had been several years, and they had yet to break ground. There was also a recording studio on the premises. We considered recording there, but Jim hadn't gotten it to work properly. I've never had a baby, so I can't speak from experience, but I believe that when a woman has a baby, she envisions the ideal site for the birth. That's similar to how I feel about recording in specific locations; I'm always looking for the ideal location to record. Jim's place was not it. He also was unprepared for our meeting. He hadn't listened to my records and didn't appear to understand who I was. So we thanked him for his time and then went.

Bo mentioned Tom Tucker, who owned a studio called Master Mix in Minneapolis. Bo had worked on numerous records with Greg Brown in that studio. Tom had also worked on big engineering projects for Prince in his studio. I loved and respected Bo, so I agreed immediately. So we scheduled a time for the entire band to meet there, and I sent the duo tape that Bo and I had recorded in Nashville to all of the musicians so they could study the songs.

Everything seemed easy and better than before. I drove my Chevrolet Silverado pickup truck all the way to Minneapolis. I've always enjoyed driving cross-country by myself. It was October, a beautiful time of year, and I watched the leaves change colours as I travelled further north. I stayed at a motel along the highway about halfway there and drove for two days.

We recorded the core recordings for Essence in roughly ten days. When we arrived in Minneapolis, we were on a tight timetable because Jim Keltner had to return to the road with Neil Young and Charlie Sexton, and Tony Garnier had to return to Dylan. As a result, there was some tinkering to be done after those individuals went, as well as a few errors that needed to be corrected without the musicians there.

Bo and I were unsure what to do. Bo proposed we bring some local Minneapolis musicians he knew into the studio for some overdubs, but I declined. So we had a little trouble figuring out how to move forward.

Tom Tucker had discovered a young man who was a wiz at Pro Tools, an early computer software used by many audio and video editors. This was my first time using Pro Tools, and this kid nailed it.

Also, I was able to speak with Charlie Sexton, who had a few days off from Dylan's tour and travelled back to Minneapolis. Those three lads rescued the day. It was similar to surgery, with Charlie, Tom, and the genius kid taking different pieces from various takes and assembling the puzzle. It was amazing what they accomplished. I had never seen anything like it. The final sound on the record was exactly what I had envisioned.

I adore that album. Today, many people approach me and tell me that Essence is their favourite of my records. I try not to have favourites, but I understand when someone does.

Essence's mixing and mastering took place between Thanksgiving and Christmas. I stayed in Minneapolis by myself. I moved from a vintage hotel to an Extended Stay hotel, where I had a suite with a kitchen. It was the first time I'd ever spent Christmas alone. I had heard that one should not spend Christmas alone, but I assumed it would be no problem for me; it was just another day.

When I was about twenty-one, my father and stepmother flew to Rome for Christmas, leaving me in New Orleans with my mother and brother. One day, Mom was into drugs and drinking, and I had to leave the apartment. I was of legal age when I walked into a bar on Christmas Eve. It was the first time I'd ever been to a pub alone. In a strange way, I felt emancipated since I no longer had to cope with my family. My father and stepmother were in another country, and my mother had gone out for the day and night. I recall thinking, "Wow, this is kind of cool in an odd sort of way." It was the first time I remember recognizing how much I appreciated being alone. And it has been true for the majority of my life.

Tom Tucker's family had looked after me over the winter months in Minneapolis while we worked on the mixes in the studio. They handed me a small Christmas tree and decorations for my hotel room. Everything was good until Christmas day. I felt a different type of melancholy than usual. The day passed so slowly. It was as if the clock was moving backwards. I made it through, but I realised I didn't want to spend the holidays alone again.

As Tom and I worked to finish Essence, Bo Ramsey was in and out of Minneapolis, helping us as required. He could simply travel back and forth from Iowa because he lived nearby. I'd had a crush on Bo for a long time, and on one of his visits, I decided to try to make something happen between us. I went out and bought candles and incense for my hotel room, ordered some delicious food and wine to be delivered, and asked him to my room to "work on the album." I carefully planned what I was going to dress and say in order to seduce him.

Bo arrived in my room, and candles and incense were lit. I had Sade playing on the boombox. My seduction attempts went entirely over his head, or beside it, or something. He showed no desire to reciprocate my romantic efforts and kept the evening solely focused on the album and our jobs.

A few years later, Bo and I crossed paths, and I reminded him that I had attempted to have sex with him. He responded, "What? Why didn't you inform me you were doing that? "I would have been delighted to oblige."

I squandered my chance. By this time, Bo had married Greg Brown's daughter Pieta. But at the very least, we had recorded a darn decent record.

Chapter 19

I hadn't seen Ryan Adams since the night he stormed out from Nashville a few years ago, but he showed up in Minneapolis while I was recording Essence. Frank Callari was still managing both of us, and Ryan came to town to play a few shows. We were all staying at the same hotel. It was an ancient mill downtown that had been transformed into a lovely vintage hotel. With all of the musicians in town, the hotel became a party hotspot.

Ryan stood in the lobby looking untidy and unruly, wearing jeans, a T-shirt, and a denim jacket, with his hair in a nasty mop. He was sitting there reading section A of The New York Times, holding the page out in front of him and completely concentrating on it. So, once again, here's the combination of attributes I find appealing: the roughneck intellectual and the poet on a motorcycle. This guy is a borderline mess, and he's reading section A of The New York Times, not the arts, sports, or business sections. Ryan saw me, put down the paper, and quickly resumed his flirtatious behaviour with me.

I had decided to make him say "I'm sorry" for abandoning me that night at the Nashville bar, never phoning me again, or responding to any of my casual overtures conveyed through Frank. Ryan was such a good boy, as if he could do no wrong, and I was going to have him say "I'm sorry." He resisted. He did not want to say it. It was like pulling teeth to get him to accept that he messed up. But he eventually did. The next day, he went to a bookstore in Minneapolis and brought me back a newly released collection of Sylvia Plath's letters, with a note to me inside.

After three days in Minneapolis, we parted ways and seldom communicated after that. That is all that happened. We've never had sex. But our interactions inspired a song. I wrote "Those Three Days," which was released on World Without Tears in 2003. It is not a verbatim account of what occurred. In fact, I still don't understand what transpired between us. People have told me they can relate to it, perhaps because it is so difficult to understand attraction.

I saw Ryan again a few years later at SXSW in Austin. We were both still handled by Frank, and we were performing at the same place on the same day. Ryan ended up on my tour bus with me, which was parked outside the arena. There were other folks around, and we spoke and drank. I was drinking Grand Marnier. There was gin and vodka nearby. Ryan and I began flirting and chatting and talking, and I completely forgot that the next morning I would be meeting the renowned photographer Annie Leibovitz for a picture shoot. I'm getting shitfaced with Ryan Adams, and I'm going to look terrible the next morning for this big shoot. I stood up to go to the restroom, and when I returned, Ryan had left. Ryan is always on point.

I somehow made it to the Hotel San José, where my band and travelling companions were staying. I passed out on the couch in my suite, still wearing my clothes. I awoke with a terrible hangover and thought, "Fuck, I've got to meet Annie Leibovitz for this photo shoot and I'm fucking hungover and looking awful." So I had a shower. I washed my hair, something I never do before a photoshoot. I learned this tip years ago: never wash your hair before a photoshoot. Leave it grimy.

Annie arrived at my San José suite precisely on schedule. When she saw me, she exclaimed, "Oh…" Then there was a long pause that seemed unpleasant. I had just gotten out of the shower and was dressed, but I hadn't applied any makeup. She responded: "I'd love to photograph you right now the way you are."

"No," I replied. "I've got a makeup artist. I have a stylist. "I have all of that." She didn't care.

"Look, Annie, I'm fucked up as shit," I said. "I'm hungover as shit and I feel like crap."

"That's okay," she said, "just do whatever you want. "Look down, look away, put on your sunglasses, pull your jacket up over your head, I don't care."

I'd never worked with a photographer who didn't make me stand there and grin even if I didn't want to. She didn't care whether I smiled or not. She understood how I felt and did not press me into another pose or position. It did not make sense to me at the time. But then I saw the photos and said, "Oh my God, this is why she is so good."

Most of the photographers I work with can tell you whether a shot is going to be nice or not while it is being taken. You cannot tell anything about Annie. She informed me that every time she photographs someone, they invariably say, "This is the worst shoot I've ever had." Nothing good is going to come out of this. Then, when they see the images, they cannot believe it.

Annie came to Nashville some time after the shoot and stopped by my house. She just wanted to hang out, which I embraced. I was renting a three-level condo, and my office was on the third floor. That's where I kept all of my books and belongings. She came up and noted that I had a copy of her legendary Rolling Stone book, which had been out for years. She says, "Oh, yeah, I pretty much fucked everybody in that book," or something to that effect. I had no idea if she was being serious. I know she's a lesbian, or perhaps she's bi. I do not know. It does not matter. People fuck each other. Whatever. Who cares?

Ryan and I didn't communicate beyond the night before the photo shoot. At the time, he was experiencing difficulties. He wasn't as dependable as a friend would be. My relationship with him was brief, yet meaningful to me. I loved him. I still do. After allegations of sexual misconduct in his past surfaced in 2019, I felt it was appropriate to contact him. I called him, and he replied, "I hope you don't think I'm a monster."

"I don't think you are a monster, Ryan," I told you. "I think you just made some bad choices."

Chapter 20

After Essence was released, we began to see some weird things on stage. I suppose I had created a fringe cult following among some of my fans. At the first Jazz Fest in New Orleans after Katrina, we were performing the song "Essence" at the House of Blues, and there was a woman off to the side of the stage openly masturbating. Security seized her and dragged her out, and she never stopped stroking herself while being hauled out. Then there was this couple who attended several of my gigs, and the man had my name tattooed on his bicep. They sent my manager a negligee with these small panties to offer me. It was the craziest thing. Otherwise, they appeared to be a normal middle-aged couple. Another person had the full lyrics to my song "Blessed" tattooed on his back, and he stepped up to the front of the stage, removing his shirt to show me. When we were playing a gig in Macon, Georgia, someone discovered where we were staying and donated a paper bag of Vidalia onions to my room. Another person wants to get my signature tattooed on him. I can go on and on. In my opinion, this type of fan attention is the ultimate honour.

After Essence, reports circulated that I was using hard substances such as heroin. I am not sure how they started. I believe it had something to do with the content of some of my songs. There are also a few references to heroin in World Without Tears. But I've never used hard drugs.

Around that time, I had a concert in Denver. I believe it was my first time playing a gig at altitude, and I was unaware of the effects. We were staying at a Kimpton Hotel, and there was an Aveda salon in the lobby offering all of these treatments. I had a fantastic massage, but you should not do it before a show; instead, do it after. After the massage, I ordered room service and drank a few glasses of wine, like I usually do before concerts. But this time, the mix of massage relaxation, altitude, and wine made me wobbly on stage. A few admirers who attended the performance posted about it online, questioning if I was high. Not long after, I was doing an interview with a journalist, and he asked, "When did you get out of rehab?"

"What?" I asked.

"You were in drug rehab, weren't you?"

"You've got the wrong person," I told you.

The closest I came to doing hard drugs was when living in Austin in 1974 or 1975. Drugs were simply flowing. You didn't even have to buy marijuana or mushrooms; they were always around, wherever you went. I was living in a house with roommates and decided to try amphetamines, which I kind of loved. A little boost for a woman who had a depressive childhood. They were small pills known as "white crosses." I'd take one of these every now and then when I was smoking marijuana, and I liked the sensation of that combination. However, I only did it for a short time. For one thing, you needed money to buy hard drugs, and I didn't have any.

When I had some extra money, I considered trying crystal meth. There was a guy in Austin who sold pure crystal meth. He reminded me of Ginger Baker, with his long hair and enormous eyes that were usually open. He was a speed fanatic, but everyone liked him since he was usually happy and upbeat. I contacted him, and he showed up at our house with a massive fucking bag of crystal meth, which terrified me. I remember thinking that the doses weren't manageable, and I had no idea how much you were meant to take. I informed him I had changed my mind. I've always felt like I have a little angel on one shoulder and a little demon on the other. This time, the little angel won. I finally stopped using harsh drugs. Over the years, I've generally settled on wine and occasionally mixed drinks.

Granted, there have been instances when I've had a little too much, just like my father and his writer pals when they hosted those literary parties at our house in Fayetteville. Even now, one of my favourite things to do is get together with a few buddies and have a few beers while breaking bread.

Chapter 21

Essence was published in June 2001, and my following album, World Without Tears, came out less than two years later, in April 2003. Throughout those years, we toured ceaselessly. I wrote World Without Tears on the journey. Those tunes just spilled out of me. My life back then was chaotic and stressful, but in a wonderful manner. My career was rising, and new chances were emerging.

I moved out of Nashville and back to Los Angeles. It was one of my restless, nomadic movements. When I wasn't touring, I lived at the Safari Inn in Burbank, a fantastic motel established in the 1950s. It had undergone extensive renovations throughout the years. It was my favourite spot to stay when I returned to Los Angeles. Normally, I could obtain the same room: an efficiency with a kitchen, a separate bedroom, and a living area. They would offer me a discounted rate for a prolonged stay. There was a decent restaurant that offered room service. That was pretty much all I needed. I'm not sure why, but staying in motels or hotels makes me feel more free-spirited. I've always fantasised about living in a hotel. I remember reading about Lauren Bacall's New York City residence, which was described as both cosy and elegant.

I turned 50 a few months before World Without Tears was released. The majority of the songs on that album were inspired by men I had brief but intense relationships with.

One of them was a bartender called Billy Mercer, whom I met at 12th and Porter near the end of my time in Nashville, the same location where I first saw Ryan Adams perform. He'd played bass in Ryan's band at one point, but he wasn't a professional musician.

I was drinking at 12th and Porter the night Joey Ramone died, and Billy was the bartender. After a time, his shift ended, and a few of us headed to another establishment called the Slow Bar. Everyone was hammered and distraught over Joey Ramone's death. We were singing Ramones songs and dancing. Billy and I ended up making out in the Slow Bar's toilet like vicious creatures. When we left, I accompanied him to his place.

Billy and I were completely incompatible—he was nineteen years younger and in a very different stage of life—but we had unbeatable chemistry. When I met him, I had no idea how young he was, and I honestly didn't care. He was soulful and, the majority of the time, sweet. He had large blue eyes and dark eyelashes. My experiences with Billy influenced the compositions "Fruits of My Labour," "Righteously," "Overtime," "Sweet Side," and "People Talkin'." However, the relationship was not progressing personally or intimately. It simply petered out.

My song "Ventura" was composed around the same time as Billy and Ryan, but it's not really about them. I composed that song with Neil Young's Everybody Knows This Is Nowhere in mind, which is one of my all-time favourite albums. To me, so much of Neil's music evokes the ocean and the sound of waves, which is unsettling. There's also a sense of isolation in his style and songs on the album. I wanted to address something like that.

Twenty years after World Without Tears was released, I was collaborating with the renowned jazz saxophonist Charles Lloyd, who told me that "Ventura" was one of his favourite songs of mine. He knew everything about me, which was flattering, but the comment about "Ventura" meant a lot because Charles is from Memphis but has spent many years in Santa Barbara, so he had a southern and Southern California mix similar to mine.

I wrote "Real Live Bleeding Fingers and Broken Guitar Strings" after spending time with The Replacements' lead vocalist, Paul Westerberg. It was another brief liaison. He had evidently been eyeing me from afar for years. In my early days in Los Angeles, I would play shows at places like Al's Bar, Raji's, and the Troubadour, and the Replacements would occasionally appear on the same weekend bill. I remember going to see them play at the Palace in Los Angeles, and they were loud, intoxicated, and great. Then, a few years later, someone sent me Paul's solo album 14 Songs, and I immediately fell in love with it and his other solo recordings.

Paul and I eventually became acquainted, and I saw him a few times when he visited Los Angeles. We communicated on the phone, and I attended his gigs. He got shitfaced drunk at one of his gigs and asked me to sit in on one of his songs. He was always fucked up. I've heard he went into recovery later. Spending time with him allowed me to get a glimpse into the life of the inebriated rock star. I remember sitting in his hotel room one time when there was a knock on the door and two giggly girls outside waiting to enter. Paul must have given them his room number backstage after the performance. I thought, "Wow, this is going to be one of those situations. I'm in my late forties, well-established, and this is happening right in front of me."

My relationship with Paul ended quickly because he was so unreliable, like a hound dog. He was a mess. But he possessed the same attributes that I usually admire: brains and talent. At one point, he was telling me about his wife and his son, and I told him, "Look, you need to go see a therapist to sort all this stuff out." He did not like that. He was very angry. I said, "See ya later." It was over.

"Atonement" was inspired by the film adaptation of Flannery O'Connor's novel Wise Blood. There's a preacher in the song, similar to my maternal grandfather, with the hellfire and brimstone, attempting to jam religion down your throat, particularly with the phrase "Lock you in a room with a holy roller and a one-man band." In Wise Blood, the main character's father is a preacher, and the character experiences frequent flashbacks.

"World Without Tears" is merely a reflection on life and pain. That's a song I usually perform when there's a national catastrophe, which seems to happen every week these days.

Stylistically, I knew I wanted World Without Tears to be more intense than anything I'd ever done. Also, The Miseducation of Lauryn Hill came out a few years ago, and I listened to it over and over. I wanted World Without Tears to have some of the traits she combined, such as hip-hop and spoken word.

With the tunes in hand, I entered the studio with my band: Doug Pettibone on guitars, Taras Prodaniuk on bass, and Jim Christie on drums. Doug and Jim both grew up on the coast, around Oxnard or Ventura, and were avid surfers. Taras grew up in the valley. These were L.A. boys through and through, and they could play nearly any genre of music.

When we started thinking about producers for the album, I was still thinking in terms of Dylan's Time Out of Mind sound. Mark Howard, an engineer, collaborated with Daniel Lanois to create the record, as well as Emmylou's Wrecking Ball and many other projects. Many of Mark's albums with Lanois were recorded in ancient New Orleans houses that had been converted into studios. Mark had recently done the same thing in Silver Lake, creating a studio in an old house, so we approached him and he agreed to work with us.

Mark's new studio was in an 18-thousand-square-foot home on a hilltop. It was erected in the 1920s by a wealthy woman who received a large sum of oil money. She was married to a silent-film actor, and they supposedly hosted large parties with guests such as Buster Keaton and Charlie Chaplin. The architecture was Spanish Mediterranean, and it was constructed by the same person who designed Beverly Hills High School and other well-known structures. There were twenty-foot ceilings and huge windows. The grounds included five acres and had three bungalows for personnel. The site previously included a citrus grove and a horse farm.

The original owners died young, and the mansion was converted into a boarding school for orphaned girls during the Great Depression. The owners then donated the property to the Immaculate Conception Home for Girls, which was operated by Catholic nuns from Mexico and remained so until the 1990s.

In the late 1990s, the sisters attempted to sell the estate but were unable to attract any purchasers because the property was so large and in such condition, and the surrounding neighbourhood was known for crime and vice.

As a result, it was the ideal location for a killer recording studio, which is precisely what Mark Howard created there.

Today, it's a boutique hotel called the Paramour. When we were recording there, it was reputed to be haunted, and I don't doubt it. For seventy years, the souls of orphaned girls lived there. Doug Pettibone slept there while we were taping and claimed to constantly hear voices and other unusual sounds. He adored it.

When the record was released, Ann Powers wrote a fantastic review that pretty much summarised the situation in her first lines:

On first listen, Lucinda Williams' latest album evokes one overarching thought: This girl is nuts. Here she is, 50 years old,

America's most respected songwriter, and she releases a disc full of snarls, mumbles, and sighs about one failed, likely sleazy romance, with songs ranging from spiritual craziness to gutter-level sorrow. The rock songs are brutal, the ballads are gory, and she even attempts to rap twice. This is not how elders are expected to behave.

Exactly. I don't clip or read many reviews, but someone pointed this one up to me, and I saved it in my scrapbook.

Looking back, Car Wheels, Essence, and World Without Tears create a sort of trilogy, though I didn't intend it that way. My career had been about taking tiny advances over time, and those three records, released over a five-year period, were the culmination of that. We recorded World Without Tears in the same way as we did Rough Trade. We went into the Paramour and just cranked the songs. We wanted it live, fresh, and gnarly. In some respects, the trilogy represents three distinct approaches to creating music about sex, love, and the status of the world—or my world.

Chapter 22

I was 51 years old, and my life and job had never been hotter. I was either on tour with my band or staying at the Safari Inn.

On March 8, 2004, we performed a sold-out event in Charlotte, North Carolina. We were backstage, and the theatre was rocking. As we were set to go onstage, a phone call came into the theatre's offices. I don't remember who called me. My mother passed away. To say I was devastated isn't enough. Every feeling imaginable surged to the surface at once. I couldn't play that show, so we had to cancel it shortly before the curtain went up. The presenter went out on stage and told the audience what had transpired, and I was later told that the audience received the news well. There was no booing or anything like that. We also had to cancel several more shows.

She was seventy-three years old, and despite having lung problems, she died unexpectedly. She had continued to reside in New Orleans until I supported her in moving into an assisted living home in Fayetteville, which I had paid for.

She had remarried a good man many years ago, an exploratory geologist. He died before she did, and she did not have a will. So, as the oldest child, I received legal power of attorney.

The tour bus took us from Charlotte to Fayetteville, a distance of about a thousand miles and approximately fourteen hours. That night, we left directly from the theatre. Of course, my father and stepmother lived in Fayetteville, and when I arrived, my stepmother was planning my mother's burial and monument. When I arrived, they went into the background and were quite encouraging.

However, when my mother's brother Cecil came, what followed was a complete nightmare for me, one of the worst events of my life. My mother did not want to spend a lot of money on her funeral. She informed me she did not want a casket and all that. She wished to be cremated and her remains placed in an urn.

When Uncle Cecil learned of my mother's death, he and his wife drove from Sulphur, Louisiana, to Fayetteville. I was in the funeral home, selecting an urn, when they stepped in. Uncle Cecil insisted on a casket, a conventional funeral, and my mother's burial in Monroe,

Louisiana, alongside her parents. That was the last thing my mother would have wanted.

The scenario was impossible. I was overcome with emotion and felt coerced into agreeing to a traditional funeral. The whole process ended up costing $11,000, which I agreed to pay. My brother and sister arrived, and the commotion just kept building, and I couldn't see through it. I was overly emotional. I ended up selecting the casket and then the vault it resides in. The funeral parlour director then asked me, "What about some of these angels?" and showed me the small ceramic angels that would be placed on each corner of the casket. He told me that my brother, sister, and I may take replicas of the angels home as keepsakes. It went on like that.

Mom's therapy was largely about coming to terms with the harm her parents and relatives had inflicted on her, something she had suffered with throughout her life. The fact that they were driving her body to Monroe to be buried with her parents was too much for me. I couldn't attend the burial.

Even today, knowing that my mother is buried where she did not want to be hurts me terribly.

My relationship with my family has been something I've spent many hours in therapy attempting to work through. My mother, near the end of her life, urged me to forgive her. So I did. I never openly shared with her what I had learnt about the sexual assault she had experienced as a child. However, knowing about it let me comprehend how difficult her emotional and psychological life had been.

My mother was mentally sick, therefore my father served as my anchor. But he had his own troubles. My family was not allowed to discuss difficulties aloud. Everything was kept within. I was never able to express my frustration or anger to anyone. Looking back, I wonder whether it would have been better if you could yell, scream, and exclaim, "Fuck you!" before slamming the door and leaving. Then the next day it's all over, and you start afresh.

My therapist refers to "frozen moments," which occur when a traumatic incident or experience becomes stuck in your psyche and causes physical symptoms such as acid reflux, migraine headaches, and so on. One of those frozen moments for me, she adds, was when my mother locked me in the closet when I was three years old because she couldn't handle normal three-year-old behaviour. She urged me to imagine this psychological terrible experience as a physical thing, and then go into that closet and talk to the little girl, soothe her, bring her out, and hold her in my arms. My therapist guided me through the activity. She told me to close my eyes and bring the little girl out of the closet, telling her she is secure, everything is OK, and she will be protected. She kept urging, "Keep holding her until you feel like she becomes one with you." In other words, the three-year-old girl and the 68-year-old woman are not separate. We are the same individual. You must enter and grab hold of the small youngster, telling her that everything will be fine. And then I became one with the tiny girl, which made me feel so much better. It was a guided visualisation state, and I informed my therapist that I didn't want my three-year-old self to vanish. She answered, "She won't vanish. She is going to join you, and you will keep her secure and okay." It is about love. You cherish that aspect of yourself, the three-year-old you. You adore her, you accept her, and she resides within you. You love her as much as you can and give her everything you own.

Looking back on my life, I can see clearly that I had a tendency to seek rough-and-tumble men who suffered from a variety of emotional issues but could also be extremely nice and brilliant, more intelligent and intriguing than the majority. Many of these males had experienced maltreatment as children, leaving them with adult issues that some may refer to as PTSD. They were emotionally unpredictable. They possessed personas that resembled Jekyll and Hyde.

I can see that my mother too suffered from this emotional condition. It had to be the result of horrific sexual assault by her father and elder brothers. As I become older, my mother's narrative irritates me even more. Her father hid behind the church's pulpit. He hid behind a Bible. He hid behind the cross. The thought of him standing up there preaching to an audience is scary and filthy. He should have been jailed. My stomach turns just thinking about how I used to sit in his lap as a child. My grandfather, someone who was meant to protect and cherish me. He ruined my mother's life. She never got a chance.

This tendency of mine reached a violent low point, or nadir, in 2004, when I returned to Los Angeles. It was around the time my mother died. My job was thriving, so you'd think I'd have outgrown this pattern—a wide spectrum of individuals were interested in me, including relatively stable folks—but such tendencies are difficult to overcome.

I held an exhibit in a winery in California, which is a gorgeous location near the shore. I spotted a crew member who was both attractive and gentle. He was like a puppy dog; Mama, may I take him home?

His name was Matthew Greeson. He was at the time residing in a sober living facility in Los Angeles. He had been there for some time and had improved enough to be able to work outside of the treatment centre. He appeared quite healthy and joyful to me. I thought, "He is sober. He is safe. He's completed a serious program and is now in good standing. He has developed, and as a result of his treatment, he has an advantage over all the other troubled males I have worked with."

I believed I didn't have to be concerned about him since he'd done the measures that most people never do: enrol in a program and straighten himself out. What I didn't comprehend was that there was a reason why he was at that treatment centre in the first place. He wasn't ready to venture out into the world yet.

I'd been around a lot of people—both men and women—who drank heavily and partied hard, but almost all of them were just wanting to unwind and have a nice time. They laughed more as they drank. They drank to have fun. For the most part, celebrants are cherry types. They wanted to forget about their concerns for a few hours without causing further problems for themselves or others.

Matthew was a distinct type. After we'd been with a while, he began imbibing here and there. He said he had it under control, and I believed him—or wanted to believe him. He was quite lovely to me at first, and I adored him for it. However, he quickly began drinking more and became aggressive about little matters. He'd become enraged at the slightest provocation. It was almost as if he had passed out while still conscious. He'd forget what he said or did the next day. The next day, he'd be doing the puppy dog thing again. He'd be quite sweet. "I'm sorry…I'm sorry."

Like so many of the males I fell for, I thought I could help him get his act together. I would advise him to continue his therapy on an outpatient basis. That is something I would encourage him through. I had no idea that these angry spirals would get to such a horrific level.

Matthew and I spent one night in Memphis at the famed Peabody Hotel. It is a large downtown hotel that has existed since the early twentieth century. The hotel has a large lobby with a fountain in the centre, and mallard ducks have lived there for decades. They swim in the fountain and go around the hotel.

I don't recall why we were in Memphis, but I do remember being fatigued and wanting to sleep. Matthew stated he was going to the bar below for a drink. So he did. When he returned to the room, he looked completely different. He became angry and nasty for no apparent cause. I wanted to get some sleep, but he had other plans for me. He wanted to engage in rough sex with me or something. I went into a complacent mentality to defend myself, appeasing and calming him down. I let him take off my clothing. We were both naked. We started wrestling. It began as a pleasant interaction, but he gradually became hostile. He shoved me down onto the bed and choked me with his arm across my chest. He grew progressively tougher. I could not move. I started to grow terrified. It was the first time I had felt so afraid around him. I feared he would murder me. I believed I may die in the Peabody Hotel.

I got the strength to crawl away from him. My fight-or-flight reflexes were kicking in hard. I was struggling for survival. I could only think of getting on the phone and calling the front desk. I went over to get the phone. He jumped on me and ripped the phone from my hands. I dashed to the door and miraculously made it out into the hallway. I was still completely naked. Matthew stormed out into the hallway, naked, and the door closed behind him, leaving us locked out without a key. I was now convinced that someone would recognize me and this would end up in a magazine. The headline read, "Lucinda Williams Was Found Naked in a Hallway in the Peabody Hotel." I was thinking: "Oh my God, my fans are going to know about this."

I crumpled up into a heap on the floor. I was seated in a foetal position, head between my knees. Matthew, for some reason, laid spread eagle on the hallway floor. Soon, a hotel security guard arrived. He opened the door and let us back into our room. Then he walked away. Back in our room, we both breathed a sigh of relief. The episode was over. I was foolish enough to believe it wouldn't happen again.

We made it back to Los Angeles, specifically to my Burbank flat. Matthew informed me he was using heroin but had it under control, which was clearly not the case. I told him he needed further treatment and competent medical help. I'm not sure why I stayed with him. I never saw him take those medicines. He was using speedballs—a mix of heroin and cocaine—in the basement of my apartment building, near the laundry area. I'd never had an intimate relationship with somebody who had used drugs like that.

Following that night, I called a friend. She handed me a copy of the AA manual, hoping that it might offer me some ideas for what I should do. Eventually, I returned Matthew to treatment. He realised he needed to leave.

I moved out of my apartment and returned to the Safari Inn by myself. The Safari Inn was always my happy place, where I felt the most protected and comfortable.

Chapter 23

I wrote the majority of the songs for my next two albums, West (2007) and Little Honey (2008), at the Safari Inn. Many of those tracks, particularly on West, are about me processing my feelings in the aftermath of my mother's death. Another way I got through it was to do as many shows as possible with Doug, Jim, and Taras, and we recorded a live album called Live at the Fillmore in 2005.

With the success of World Without Tears and expanding prospects for me, Luke Lewis at Lost Highway handed me a half-million-dollar budget for my next album. I reserved some time at the Radio Recorders studio in Hollywood, where Frank Sinatra had made many of his records, and I recorded samples of twenty-four songs I had composed at the Safari Inn.

I also met my hubby in 2005. One night, I went to the notorious Whisky a Go Go in Hollywood to witness Hank Williams III, the grandson of Hank Williams, who was blending punk and country in an unusual way. I was standing in the crowd when a man named Damien came up to me and offered to trim my hair. He handed me his business card. A few days later, I took him up on his offer and scheduled an appointment for a good friend of mine, Shilah Morrow, as a birthday present. Hairroin, a salon in Hollywood near Sunset and Vine, was suitably called. Damien had already begun working on Shiloh's hair when he excused himself for a moment to meet his final appointment of the day, who was just walking in. I looked up and noticed a tall, lean man with a broad smile and bright blue eyes. His smile revealed a shining silver tooth, which I adored. Damien introduced us. His name was Tom Overby, and he told me we had a mutual friend named Bonnie Butler from Minneapolis. He had recently relocated to Los Angeles from Minneapolis, where he was the music buyer for Best Buy. He had landed a position at Fontana, a record label owned by Universal, in Los Angeles.

Shilah and I had planned to see a friend of ours, Susan Mitchell, sing a block away at the Hotel Cafe later that night, but we had some time before then, so we headed to the Velvet Margarita for a drink. Tom joined us, and we drank some tequila at the Velvet Margarita, a popular Hollywood Mexican restaurant with velvet Elvises and Day of the Dead folk art. After a few tequilas and tortilla chips, we went to the Hotel Cafe. A while later, I was feeling the tequila and realised I shouldn't drive home, so Tom offered to bring me home to the Safari Inn. I was smitten.

Soon after we met, I offered Tom to come over to Radio Recorders after he left his Universal office to listen to my new tracks. Even before we met, Tom had attentively listened to all of my records. He carefully listened to everyone's records. That is what he does. We purchased a good bottle of wine and sat down to listen to all of the songs. Tom exclaimed, "I'm completely blown away. This is another step forward in your music. If you put all of these on one album, it'll be your Exile on Main Street."

A few while later, Tom asked if I wanted to see Bruce Springsteen at the Pantages Theatre in Hollywood. It was the Devils & Dust Tour, and Springsteen was performing solo in smaller theatres. Tom said he could obtain seats, but I said, "Hold on, I'll call Frank Callari," and I did. We soon received tickets and backstage passes.

Bruce's performance was amazing, and we went backstage afterward. It was quite the scene. Jim Carrey came up to me and raved about my music. We met Sam Moore from the renowned Sam & Dave. There were some familiar faces, including T-Bone Burnett and his wife, Callie, as well as my old friend Jesse Malin, the singer of the legendary New York punk band D Generation. Bruce approached me and asked, "Hey, Lu, how ya doin'?" I was a little overwhelmed and had problems speaking, but I think I said something reasonable because a few minutes later, after the crowd thinned out, Bruce approached me and Tom and offered us food. We headed to Kate Mantilini's popular West Hollywood eatery. It was Bruce, T-Bone and Callie, Jesse, the Edge of U2 and his wife, and me and Tom, whom I'd only known for a few weeks. It was exhilarating, but also breathtaking and unearthly. Bruce kept trying to start a discussion with me, and while I struggled at first, I eventually got there. All night, I kept thinking about whether you call the Edge "the Edge" in person or just "Edge," and whether he has a street name. What does his wife call him? The truth is that they were wonderful individuals, and I should not have been so frightened.

Bruce eventually got up and said he had to leave, but everyone was invited to stay and the money was paid. When he came up to me and Tom to say goodbye, Tom told Bruce, "I read an interview with you several years ago where you claimed that rock and roll reached down into your house and pulled you out, and I just want to tell you that you did the same for me. I wouldn't be sitting here right now if not for you."

Bruce leaned over and hugged Tom, who replied, "Thanks, man, that really means a lot."

On the way back home, I told Tom, "That was really sweet, what you said to Bruce and how you said it." He was still a man I didn't know well, but I had a sense he'd be around for a while.

On our third date, we went to see Jason Molina and his band Magnolia Electric Co. at a dive in Echo Park. Tom introduced me to Molina's music, and I got smitten with his albums. I would like to cover some of his songs someday. I recall Tom and I discussing album sales or personal money that night, and he stated, "I'm good with numbers," which I thought was really cool. He also had the appropriate amount of bling. I had never been around a man like him before.

On our first "date," we listened to my new tunes at Radio Recorders. Our second date was a night with Bruce and his pals. Then comes Jason Molina's concert. Not a bad start for what turned out to be a wonderful and long-lasting marriage.

Tom became an intimidating new presence in my life. He wasn't one of those down-and-out poet-motorcycle-bad-boy types who could barely keep it together. He was really brilliant. He also has the capacity to recognize that when I'm in a bad mood, it's just that; it's not a problem that has to be confronted, questioned, or avoided. He accepts the situation. A few years after I met Tom, tensions were running high during a recording session at Village Recorders on Santa Monica Boulevard. I had a meltdown and ran out of the studio, disappearing. I walked throughout the neighbourhood. I'd done this before. Tom came out and scoured the streets looking for me. He was phoning and texting me, but I was not responding. I had circled several blocks numerous times, and Tom was still phoning and messaging me. He said he was afraid. It wasn't a bad neighbourhood for a lady to stroll about late at night, but it also wasn't fantastic.

Finally, I answered.

"What?"

"What do you mean by 'what'? "Where are you?"

"Over here."

"Over where?"

"Behind you."

Tom turned around to see me standing kitty-corner from the studio, under a streetlight in front of Floyd's Barbershop. I knew he would always be by my side.

Chapter 24

A few years after I began dating Tom, Rolling Stone published an article in which I indicated that I was seeing him. Tom was working at Universal at the time, and he claims that after reading the Rolling Stone article, several of his colleagues approached him and said something like, "Be careful, our reps at her label tell us that she's literally insane." Tom was astute enough to recognize that many male artists make artistic judgments similar to mine, yet they are not labelled as nuts. He recognizes that women have been treated differently for millennia.

I knew I wanted to marry Tom. He was unlike anyone I'd ever been with in terms of intelligence and kindness. It is something you feel. You simply know. This is it.

Tom and I shared a tour bus in 2006. We lived in Los Angeles, and the bus was in Nashville. It was a short tour, just me and Doug Pettibone on guitars, with my father reading a few poems.

"You want to go shopping for diamonds?" Tom asked me on the bus. That is how he proposed. Tom claims that I stated that, not him. He claims I asked, "When are you gonna get me a diamond?" That isn't how I remember it. We joke about it now.

The following show after Nashville took place two days later in Minneapolis. Tom mentioned that he knew a terrific jewellery store in Omaha, which was on the way to Minneapolis. We rode the bus to Omaha and stayed overnight in the parking lot adjacent to the jewellery store, giving us plenty of time to make a selection when the store opened the next day.

Unfortunately, my OCD kicked in that morning when I realised I'd have to make a decision on the ring. I wanted to make a decision because I adored Tom, but I was also feeling overwhelmed. I was really nervous. I struggled to get dressed to go to the supermarket. It took hours. I was a nervous wreck. It was far more nerve-racking than doing a show. I would have done everything to get my mind off choosing a ring. I said to Tom: "You're getting a good look at my neurotic side."

"I've seen it many times before," he explained.

"Do you still want to marry me?" I asked.

"Yes, I do," he replied.

Finally, twenty minutes before the store closed, we entered. There were plenty of possibilities. I knew I didn't want a ring with a large, fat diamond jutting out. I wanted one with diamonds placed within the band. There was a "don't touch anything" atmosphere throughout the store. I felt as if everyone was looking at me. "Make a decision, lady, make a decision."

I've made a decision. We were formally engaged. We boarded the bus and went to the next tour stop in Minneapolis.

Not long after, Tom suggested to me, "Let's get married onstage," which I thought was a fantastic idea. Then we agreed to do it at First Avenue, a well-known club in Minneapolis where I had previously performed. Tom is from there, so it seemed like a decent spot to do it. The clincher was when I told my father about our proposal, he remarked, "That's great. "Hank Williams got married onstage."

It took a few years to include First Avenue into our tour program. We eventually married on September 18, 2009 (9-18-9). It corresponds to one of my life-path numbers in numerology terms. I can be a touch New Agey, which traces back to my time working in health food stores. Nine is the month. One and eight equal nine. The year was nine.

It ended up being a beautiful day. We all stayed at a hotel across the street from First Avenue. We rented out a restaurant on the next block. Everything was within walking distance. It was a large party.

We had invited roughly half of the audience—friends who had flown into town for the play and wedding. The other half had no idea they were going to witness a wedding. I believe some of my fans may have heard stories about it.

Tom and I purchased a house in Studio City about a year and a half before our wedding. We still live in that house, though we alternate between Los Angeles and Nashville.

In 2010, my stepmother, Jordan, wrote me a letter informing me that my father had been diagnosed with Alzheimer's disease. She was beside herself. I remember her telling me that she had no idea if she was spelling the word correctly. In addition to the letter, she provided Still Alice, a book about Alzheimer's. Lisa Genova's story is about a woman named Alice who has an early-onset variant of the condition. The novel's message is that the lady who was Alice is still alive, even if pieces of her appear to be gone as time passes. But Alice is still there.

Later that year, Tom and I travelled to Fayetteville to visit my father and stepmother for the Christmas holidays. My father and I were alone in the sunroom off the main room of our house. Jordan must have been asleep upstairs. We'd had our usual evening of sipping wine, talking, and listening to music. My father was still able to keep it together when we were present. But that night, he told us something that struck me like a ton of bricks. He informed us that his sickness had deteriorated to the point where he could no longer write poetry or read it publicly in public. To me, it was the most heartbreaking thing he could say. "Honey, I can't write anymore." It was like stating he couldn't see or speak anymore.

He had lost a significant portion of himself. That's how sickness works. Things fade, break off, disintegrate, and perish gradually. It was painful to watch that part of him vanish. The sickness had harmed a part of him that was essential to his identity.

That night, I took a yellow legal pad and wrote him a lengthy note, which I put on the kitchen table for him to read in the morning. I informed him that even though he could no longer write poetry, he remained a poet.

The next morning, he told me the note had moved him. He gave me a hug and thanked me. He also informed me that the note was well written. Always the instructor.

Over the next four years, my father would gradually lose the remainder of himself. In late 2014, he was transferred to an assisted living memory care unit, where he died on January 1, 2015.

It wasn't lost on me that Hank Williams died on New Year's Day, too. I was born in the month and year 1953.

Made in the USA
Thornton, CO
07/08/24 17:35:41

b3c58a70-027a-4001-887d-da787af5c828R01